SONG, DANCE, AND CUSTOMS
OF PEASANT POLAND

SONG, DANCE, AND CUSTOMS
OF PEASANT POLAND

BY

SULA BENET

WITH A PREFACE BY
MARGARET MEAD

POLISH HERITAGE PUBLICATIONS

To Ruth Benedict
My teacher and friend

Polish Heritage Publication, 1996 edition.
Republished by permission of Roy Publishers.

Copyright© 1951, 1996.

For information, address:
POLISH HERITAGE PUBLICATIONS
75 Warren Hill Road
Cornwall Bridge, CT 06754

Distributed to the book trade by:
HIPPOCRENE BOOKS, INC.
171 Madison Avenue
New York, NY 10016

Library of Congress Cataloging-in-Publication Data

Benet, Sula, 1903-
        Song, dance, and customs of peasant Poland / by Sula Benet ;
with a preface by Margaret Mead.
                p.   cm.
        Originally published: New York : Roy Publishers, 1951.
            ISBN 0-7818-0447-7 (alk. paper)
            1. Poland--Social life and customs--1945- 2. Peasantry--Poland.
    I. Title.
    DK4437.B46   1996   96-13450
    305.5'633' 09438--dc20   CIP

CONTENTS

LIST OF ILLUSTRATIONS

PUBLISHER'S PREFACE

IN THE 1930s Sula Benet, then a student at the University of Warsaw, began to study the life of Polish peasants, a subject which led to many field trips before and after World War II.

Concentrating on the regions of present day Poland, the author presented a basic portrait of peasants and peasant ways throughout the diverse, elastic and curiously consistent area that is Poland. "Nevertheless," says the author, "The values and to some extent the specific customs described here are shared by all Poles."

Since its publication in 1951, the book has become a cherished classic for all students of Polish life and lore, and is now being reprinted as a tribute to the author and her enduring work.

In the Preface to the book, Margaret Mead, the famous American anthropologist, said of the work: "It is a task of gentleness and fine detail, to piece together again the relationship of one civilization to another, of the past to the present, of the country to the city, of ways that were to ways that will be. This book is a real contribution..."

Out of print for some time, *SONG, DANCE AND CUSTOMS OF PEASANT POLAND* will be a treasured addition to every home library of families interested in enduring Poland.

PREFACE

TO EACH PERSON in the modern world there has come a new need to think over his or her relationships, to the past and to the future, to the nation of which one is now a part, and to that nation or nations from which one's forbears, within memory, came. Some European valley which fifty years ago seemed cut off from the affairs of the United States so firmly that its only connection was to send one family—or perhaps ten families—to settle in Massachusetts or Ohio, may have recently been a battle-ground for men from these states. If one's own grandparents did not come from there, one examines with new eyes those neighbours who share that particular tradition because their grandparents did. So in the United States, to each one of us, with the tightening of communications, with the enclosing of the once distant and little known places of the earth into one newly born and as yet uneasy neighbourhood, there comes a new desire to know something of our own origins, and of the origins of our friends and relatives in law who stem from different stock.

This is a repetition on a spatial scale of what happened in many parts of Europe, when the intelligentsia, bred of the new cities and of the new life in the cities, stirred uneasily, and looked back at the people whom they had left in the villages. Where one generation impatiently attempted to shake off the fetters of tradition—often labelling them as supersition—their children and grandchildren, seeking to weave together the national life into a continuous self-con-scious thread, sought again these same folkways and folk beliefs, making them contribute in a new way to a whole view of life. The piece of embroidery on a peasant dress, a special kind of bread at Easter, a dance step, a greeting or a

way of planting grain—details which had once bound together the life of peasants who lived from spring to spring
within the narrow confines of their village, were lifted up, to
provide motifs for architecture, or patterns for new patriotic
rituals, now not for a single village or region, but for a whole
people.

This process of finding again, at a different level, the
special characteristic beauty of the traditional ways of life of
the peasantry, was, Dr Benet tells us in this book, particularly
important in Poland, in Poland with its genius for fusing
every event of life into a deeply felt national ideal. And in
this book, Dr Benet, originally educated in Poland as a
student of local tradition and folklore, later came to the
United States and learning American ethnological approaches, has given us just such a picture of the life of the
Polish peasantry, in its ritual and symbolic aspects. A first
book, it preserves much of her European way of looking at
things, but also includes enough of an American approach
to make it easily intelligible to the reader who is more
American than Polish, but who is nevertheless interested in
Poland.

This book is not the whole story of the life of the peasantry.
Each people selects those aspects of the life of the people
which fit into their growing contemporary conception of
themselves. In one country, the poverty of the masses may be
of greatest symbolic importance, in another, their sturdy
resistance to change, in a third, their intuitive knowledge of
the human heart, in a fourth, their laughter. Dr Benet has
set down here the story of fasts and feasts, of stern hardship
and occasional great gaiety, of ploughing and planting,
saint's day and ritual precaution, an account as vivid and as
concrete as the paper inlays which the Polish peasants made
so cleverly. It is a picture of the Polish peasants labouring
many days for the few on which they dress for marriage or

for harvest festival and dance, dance with vigour in spurts of gaiety which gave them rare, but sure, release from the toil which was their every day lot.

There are other themes, some of which I hope Dr Benet will write someday. But this book is a fitting transition from her world of Polish scholarly study of peasant lore and custom to modern America with its attempts to make scientific studies of national character. Many of the notes and pictures she brought with her when she came, others she gathered on return visits. Their meaning became deepened as she talked to Americans of Polish background, who showed an interest and a need for information that she could not have guessed in Poland.

So, Dr Benet has given us a book about the stern hardships and the vivid ceremonial aspects of peasant life, as it existed up through World War II, seen in double perspective, from the intellectual life of a Polish University (Warsaw), and from the intellectual life of an American University (Columbia), seen through eyes accustomed to the Polish countryside and re-seen for the eyes of those Americans who have never seen Poland and so must conjure up, as best they may 'The thatched white cottage with the bright red window frames', 'the Christmas tree, festooned and tinselled, hanging head down from the most honoured corner of the room', 'the Lenten herring dragged through the village to an ignominious burial', 'the matchmaker with the flower boutonniere, ceremonial sash, and the vodka bulging from his pocket', 'the great stove reigning in the corner of the dimly lit room and sending its smoke up to envelope the fantastic paper "spider" on the ceiling', 'the Easter table decked with greenery, loaded with masterpieces for the stomach and eye —the lofty *babka*, the roasted meats, the sprightly border, the paschal lamb carved in butter, the patterned, painted eggs', 'the mountaineer, gigantic in the firelight, tossing his long-handled axe as he leaps high in the brigands' dance'.

B

In this modern world where so many ties have been broken, where people have moved, not a day's walk, but a day's flight apart, where children so often never hear the sound of the speech in which their own parents were lulled to sleep, it is a task of gentleness and fine detail, to piece together again the relationship of one civilization to another, of the past to the present, of the country to the city, of ways that were to ways that will be. This book is a real contribution to this new fabric which is so urgently needed.

Margaret Mead

American Museum of Natural History
January 1, 1951

INTRODUCTION

THIS BOOK IS an attempt to give the flavour and the colour of Polish peasant life. It is devoted to only one segment—though by far the largest—of the Polish population. Nevertheless, the values and to some extent the specific customs described here are shared by all Poles.

The Polish tradition, and its manifestation in folk life, have survived to an amazing extent, despite the upheaval of the war years, the post-war dislocations, and the increasing urbanization of the country. The cowpaths of old have changed to roads of cobble-stone or cement; thatched roofs are gradually giving way to shingled roofs; new houses and cottages are apt to be built of brick instead of wood; a passing automobile is no longer a rarity. Nevertheless, many of the old customs persist and even when they disappear much of the old feeling for them remains. By the peasants as well as by the intelligentsia, folk customs are often cherished through affection and pride, quite aside from belief in their particular necessity.

Three times Poland has been wiped off the map. Yet there is still a Poland, precisely because it is part of being Polish to oppose national invasion and occupation by clinging stubbornly to the national folkways and traditional behaviour. A collection of Polish folk customs and folklore, therefore, is not merely a collection of supersitions observed by the folk for the sake of practical results. It is also a record of national self-expression deliberately cultivated as an expression of patriotism and the will to survive.

The wide variations in custom found in different localities will be suggested in the present account, but with no pretence at geographical precision in cataloguing them. The

strong core of continuity through time and through space
is as characteristic as is the rich gamut of modifications
introduced by regions, by towns, by individuals. What is
presented, then, is not a blueprint but rather a basic portrait
of peasants and peasant ways throughout the diverse,
elastic, and curiously consistent area that is Poland.

The area covered is that of present day Poland, including the
virtually homogeneous population that represents basic Polish
culture, and excluding the eastern portions of pre-war Poland
—Ruthenia and White Russia—which are now part of the
U.S.S.R.

The portrait has been drawn on the basis of study continued through many years. As a student of anthropology in
the University of Warsaw, the author did fieldwork (1930-31)
among the peasants, as observer and as participant, in many
villages in varied regions of the country. Later, in the United
States, some of the material collected in Poland was used for
newspaper articles and it was the response to these articles
that first made evident the need for a fuller account of Polish
life. Continuing study in anthropology brought new perspective on the familiar lifeways. Subsequently it was possible to
return to Poland in 1938 and again in 1948 and 1949 for
further field-work, enriched by new methods of study and
new insights. The last two trips were made possible by grants
from the Social Science Research Council, the Anthropology
department of Columbia University, and from the Buell
Quain Fund.

The author's greatest debt is due to Dr Ruth F. Benedict,
as teacher, as friend, as inspiration. My deepest appreciation
and thanks go to Mrs Elizabeth Herzog whose keen understanding of the Polish culture was of invaluable help in the
preparation of the manuscript. She assisted in analysing the
material, in contributing additional insights, in organizing the
book and in the final writing. To Dr Margaret Mead are

offered special thanks for her help and encouragement, as an individual and as Director of the Columbia University Project, Research in Contemporary Cultures.

Great thanks are due to a number of people who read the manuscript with care and contributed constructive criticisms and suggestions: especially to Mr Peter P. Yolles, Drs Alexander Herz, Vincenty Natkanski, Irene Rozeney, and Mrs Helen Zand. To all my Polish friends in Poland, who helped me to collect and to evaluate my material, I offer my warmest thanks, and my hope that they will recognize in it a true portrait of the people they understand so well.

I POLAND'S PEASANTS

Matthew is dead
And laid out on the board,
But if they would strike up a tune for him
He would dance;
For such is the soul of Mazur
That though dead
He will not be still.

You ride to the notary on feathers, but
you trudge back from the notary on foot.

THE POLISH PEASANT, like most humans, is a compound
of paradoxes. They are not contradictions, any more than
summer is a contradiction of winter. The contrasts and
extremes that he displays are sometimes striking but they are
all very much part of the whole.

He is proud, fiery; and he is oppressed. He is poor in
worldly wealth, rich in finery and display. His routine is a
round of arduous toil, broken by an amazing number of
holidays and festivals. His behaviour is bound by the most
rigid etiquette and decorum, yet includes frequent bursts of
fury and brawling. His credo is sternly moralistic, even
Puritan, but it makes room for grand and unapologetic
abandon in love, in the dance, at times in his cups.

He is realistic, hard-headed, sensible; and at the same time
brimming over with magical rites and beliefs. He has an
overwhelming interest in legal procedures—and is remarkably ready to take the law into his own hands. He has been,
through the centuries, a prey to the elements and to human
tyranny, yet he retains always some sense of being able to
control his own fate.

The belief that he can rule his own life is rooted in the
conviction that, despite any fate or any oppressor, he can
rule himself. He has been brought up with a strict insistence

on self discipline. The hard spirit, *hart ducha*, represents to him the pinnacle of virtue; 'Pawn yourself but stand up' is the rule that has been ingrained since infancy. Linked to the insistence on self-discipline is an almost fanatic concern with 'honour', with independence and with status—the attributes by which a man shows that his spirit is hard and his self-command absolute.

All these qualities must take visible form, and for a peasant all of them are rooted in the land. A man without land lacks status and dignity to an extent that places in jeopardy his independence and his 'honour'. His standing in the community grows out of the soil he owns.

It is not income that counts, but acres. The more land, the higher the status—'No one ever has too much of goods and lands', says the proverb. To be born into a land-owning family, however, is better than to buy land.

The word *gospodarz* means peasant landowner, and it is used as a title of address for those who merit it. One says 'Gospodarz . . .' in greeting a landowner, and addresses his wife as 'Gospodyni . . .' A man without claim to that title is a man without roots and without stature. The *komorniki*, who are tenant farmers living on another's land, are rated as the humblest people in the village, perhaps just a little better than beggars.

The peasant is not alone in the value he places on land ownership. Successful professional people or rich merchants, whenever they can put money aside, will buy land so that they can be called landowners, *ziemianie*. This adds splendour to their position.

Since the great dream is to own land, and more land, country boys do not yearn for the city. On the contrary, those who do go to work in towns are apt to look and work toward the day when they can return and have a holding of their own. Often when they go abroad it is with the idea of returning to establish a farm in their native village. Some who stay abroad sacrifice and plan in order to acquire land and a house 'back home', even though they never expect to occupy it.

It is very rare for a man to sell his land of his own free will in order to move into a more profitable occupation. Despite the increasing hardships of farm life, the prestige of land ownership has meant more than pecuniary gain. To be a landowner, a *gospodarz*, is automatically the peasant's ambition.

For a peasant to lose his land means to lose his dignity, his independence and a large part of his honour. Accordingly, the darkest day of a peasant's life is apt to be the one on which he retires in favour of his sons, giving up his title to the land and with it his title to much that for him represents adulthood and manhood.

His retirement is brought about by the system of marriage settlement and inheritance. Each time a son marries, the father makes over to him a portion of the farm. Ordinarily the result is that when the last son marries, the father is left landless, or virtually so. This usually happens when he is past the peak of his strength but still far from decrepit—between fifty and sixty.

From the moment he writes over his property, a man has absolutely no control in it. He has not even a share of its proceeds, unless a modest one is stipulated in the contract— and sometimes not even then.

It is considered his duty to turn the farm over to younger and stronger hands and if he hesitates too long the pressure of public opinion, combined with family pressure, may force him to do so. The duty is accepted as an evil necessity, despite the frequent saying, 'I have worked enough in my lifetime, now I may retire on my children.' For every peasant knows how often such retirement means retiring to a bed of thorns, or perhaps in the end to no bed at all.

Upon dividing their property, the parents settle with the son or daughter in whom they have the greatest confidence, with the provision that they shall be supported until death. This provision is called *dozywocie,* support for life, and carries with it an additional share of property or money.

The whole arrangement is elaborately specified in a contract, which at times provides also that the parents are to receive a given allowance in kind. A certain amount of grain, potatoes, cabbage, may be allotted to them so that they will not be entirely dependent on the whim of their children.

As the very existence of the contract suggests, the lot of retired parents may be harsh. Often they are viewed as a burden on their children, a drain on the meagre board, an encumbrance in cramped quarters—so often that it is not uncommon to include in the contract a clause binding the children to honour their aged parents, under threat of losing parental and divine blessing.

The threat is not always enough. Since the farmer retires at about fifty, the duty of supporting him may burden his filial host for twenty or thirty years, causing endless lawsuits.

Up to a point the necessary evil is accepted with the grim realization that, as the proverb puts it, 'old age is not happiness and death is not bliss'. But if parents are still strong, they may prefer to go out and beg their bread rather than depend on the mercy of merciless children. Shame is believed to fall on the children who made begging necessary, and to shame them is often the parents' purpose. Such revenge is for the most part flimsy; however, the pangs of humiliation are not strong enough to prevent frequent additions to the ranks of the beggars.

The retirement custom, whereby a man in the prime of life is under social compulsion to convert himself into a dependent, if not a beggar, is widely accepted, with whatever reluctance. Its importance and impact are evidenced in numerous proverbs and tales. Whatever its toll, it is so strongly entrenched that in some cases the custom has been continued—with appropriate local modifications—even after immigration to the United States.

It is the ride to the notary to draw up the retirement contract that is referred to in the saying, 'You ride to the notary on feathers but you trudge back from the notary on foot'.

The grim picture of farmer abdication should be offset by one that marks the other extreme of the gamut. The peasant's life, like most others, is lived chiefly in the middle range, and if there are occasional extremes of gloom there are also flashes of gaiety. None is more gay or more characteristic than the folk dancing. It is appropriate that the music for the National Anthem, *Poland is Not Yet Lost*, is a melody taken from the mazurka. For dancing is an important national pastime, the hub of recreational activity; and the mazurka, in its variegated forms, is the most popular Polish dance.

The dancing is not done with the legs and arms alone, but with the whole being. And it is not a loose thread of activity, but is woven into the fabric of community life. To be a good dancer is to be a popular person, even after the music stops. Nor is dancing for young people only. Even old women may decide to join in, though old men are more apt to hang back.

No full-fledged social gathering is complete without dancing, and no dance is complete without singing. All the dance tunes have words which the onlookers sing, and often the dancers too. But the mazurka takes all the dancers' breath and leaves none over for more than an occasional 'hop, hop'.

The onlookers become part of the dance, singing, stamping, preening in their finery—for every social gathering is a welcome opportunity to 'dress up'. The colours of the costumes are as vivid as the music. Ribbons fly, striped or flowered skirts swish, brilliant headdresses sway, buckles gleam.

If there is room for more than one couple, they line up ready for the mazurka. The leader starts—there is always a leader in Polish group dances—followed by the next in order, and then the next, until all are in action. The woman circles about her partner while he crouches or leaps. In this, as in most dances, the woman's field of activity is limited. She is the helpmeet, playing the supporting role to the performing male. The field for improvisation is his. But if he is really skilful he knows how to keep his partner in the dance so that she is a joint performer and not merely a background for his solo. He will turn to her, take her hand, involve her in his feats, and leave her a-tiptoe for his immediate return.

Because it seems the essence of dance—fire and gaiety, the mazurka has been adopted by dancers of many countries. But none can fly through its measures like the native Pole. All that is most sparkling in him, and least likely to be imitated, seems caught in its rhythmic, sharply punctuated measures.

Between the glamour of the peasant's dance and the gloom of his abdication lie all the shadings and mutations that make up the rounded cycle of his life. It is not an easy life for any peasant in Poland, even the most prosperous. It imposes on all a rule of hard work.

In this life, work, religion and recreation are inseparable. Every phase of sowing, tending, and reaping the crops carries its share of religious belief and observance, and on the other hand much of the social activity comes through the crop climaxes and the religious festivals that celebrate them.

Everyone goes to church each Sunday, the young girls carrying their prayer books, the women walking sedately behind their husbands. Moreover, one dresses for church as for a minor party, and one looks forward to mingling and gossiping after services, since the church is social centre as well as house of worship.

Until World War II, Poland was overwhelmingly Catholic, and to be a Pole has been regarded as synonymous with being a Catholic. With the possible exception of Rumania and Italy, no country in Europe celebrates so many religious holidays, most of them related to the agricultural cycle. Except for weddings, these agro-religious festivals furnish the high spots of social life. Traditionally the peasant has had little interest outside his home, except the Church.

In religion alone the Poles have displayed unanimity. There have been no dissident sects. Emphasis is not on points of doctrine, or on mystical content, but on concrete observance. The peasants are devout, but their piety is practical rather than theoretical. They are concerned with the Deity and the Saints as living beings who can help or harm, not as the embodiment of abstract principles. Their relationship with these beings in concerned with specific behaviour rather than with general attitudes and tenets. The peasant is a realist in a world where saints, ghosts and black magic have as much reality as the barley in his field and the cow in his stable.

II THE PEASANTS' POLAND

Tempo di Mazurka

POLAND IS SET in the very centre of Europe. Geographically, economically, and to a great extent culturally, she has been a highway between the eastern and the western halves of the continent.

Her geographical position made her for centuries one of the important east-to-west trade routes of Europe, and a flourishing power in the international trade of the Middle Ages. But it also became a source of endless trouble, since her frontiers stood wide open, with no natural barriers except the mountains along the southern border.

Few states of modern times have had a more varied history. Squeezed in between three great powers, her boundaries have been battered through the years, as Germans in their *Drang nach Osten* and Russians in the drive to the West have advanced or receded. The perpetual swaying of these ever-debated frontiers is responsible for Poland's most difficult and dangerous minority problems. But while the outer rims have fluctuated, the core of the country, in the basin of the Vistula, has remained constant.

The combination of central consistency and surface variety is characteristic also of Polish culture. Swept by converging streams of economic, political and social events, Poland has been affected by all. Yet she has remained stubbornly unique. Looking to the West and leaning toward the East, she has absorbed much, resisted much, and remained very much herself. In many respects, Poland presents a remarkable example of continuity not often met with in history.

The survival of any national entity is impressive in view of the fact that from 1795 to 1918 there was no Poland on the map. During those years she was partitioned between Germany, Russia and Austria, and the marks of the occupying countries remain clearly recognizable in the portions they dominated.

The Roman Catholic Church, more than a thousand years old in Poland, is still the faith of more than ninety-five percent of the Polish people. Most of the others are members of the Lutheran, Methodist, and other Protestant churches. The Jews of Poland, before the war, numbered three and a half millions, but the German policy of systematic extermination reduced that number to about one hundred and fifty thousand.

Predominantly, Poland is a plain—by definition, since that is the meaning of *Pole*. It is a vast plain and a variegated one, with rolling lowlands to the North and raised plateaux in the South; with two large rivers and innumerable small ones, threading a network of water throughout the land. Today the country is bounded on all sides by natural frontiers: the Baltic Sea on the north, the Bug River on the east, the Oder and the Nysa Rivers on the west. The southern boundary is outlined by the great rugged range of the Carpathians, and this strip of mountain region supplies contrast in culture as well as in topography. Appropriately, the Polish mountain stretch is sub-divided into segments that are part of a single culture area, yet each distinct in itself. The total area encompassed is one hundred and twenty thousand square miles, about the size of New Mexico.

Although industry has increased rapidly in recent years, the vast majority of the Polish people live on the soil, literally as well as economically. Almost half the total land area is cultivated, and until 1938 almost three-fourths of the population was rural. Since the second World War, industry has advanced rapidly, so that the census of 1946 showed a somewhat smaller proportion settled in rural communities— about sixty-eight per cent of the total which in that year numbered not quite twenty-four million. The main crops are rye, potatoes, oats, wheat, barley and sugar beets. Dairy farming and stock raising are also very important.

In this land of farmers, there are still hardly more than half a dozen important cities and large towns. Most of the people live in the thousands of small towns and villages, few very large and few very small, averaging five hundred to one thousand inhabitants. Isolated farms are very rare.

The villages vary in appearance, according to their location, yet their composition is similar. The settlement is the nucleus around which the fields are spread. In the most typical villages, the houses are built along two sides of a long road, with the fields lying behind them. In some places, the houses cluster about an open common, and the fields ray out from that centre. Each house has a little garden and farm buildings.

A feature common to all villages is the roadside shrine or cross that gives a characteristic colour to the Polish land-scape. Each village has at least one, and sometimes more. The shrine is usually located at the very edge of the village, establishing a boundary line. A popular place is at the cross-roads, because more people pass here and also because cross-roads are believed to be a favourite haunt of evil spirits, who may be held in check by the beneficent influence of a sacred figure. The passer-by will stop to rest and pray at the shrine, and perhaps to leave an offering of flowers or green boughs. Such shrines are usually walled in on three sides and roofed with shingles or wide planks topped with a small tower, a glazed pottery ball or a decorative iron cross. Sometimes the stump of an old tree will be hollowed and protected by a railing. The most ancient of these shrines contain seated figures of Christ, with his head resting on his hand, called 'the Troubled Jesus'.

The shrine that marks the village limits, often marks also the parting of the ways. When an honoured guest from outside takes his leave, the hosts may accompany him as far as the shrine; or when a son goes to serve his military term, his parents may go with him to this point. When a corpse is carried to the cemetery on his last journey from home, part of the funeral cortege may take leave of him at the shrine, rather than at the grave.

On occasion, the roadside shrine may become the scene of official village action, a sanctified open air town hall. In time of drought, people gather here to offer up prayers for rain— an activity initiated by the group rather than the Church. In olden days if the village took the law into its own hands and administered punishment, it would be meted out under the roadside cross.

Any sizeable village will of course include a church, which will also serve the smaller settlements in the neighbourhood. The priest is an important personage, less than a member of the nobility but far loftier than the peasants. Below the priest, but still above the peasants is the organist, who is, in a sense, the social secretary of the church. A really small village will probably have neither church nor school, and sometimes it is necessary to go five or six kilometres to reach one; but however far it is, the peasant will go there every Sunday.

Most villages have their own blacksmith and cobbler, and usually a little inn, perhaps also housing a store. There may also be a local miller and a small grocery store. Otherwise people buy their supplies at the fairs.

The village is, up to a point, a self-governing unit, and

c

local self-government in some form has a long history in Poland. As a rule, each village has its own assembly or *gromada*, but it may happen that a few small settlements are combined into one *gromada*. Every citizen, of either sex, has the right to take part in the assembly if twenty-four years old and in residence for at least a year. The *gromada* controls communal possessions: pasturelands, woods, money. Its properties vary, according to the region and the prosperity of the local populace.

Villages with fewer than two hundred inhabitants are governed by a *Soltys*, elected by the *gromada* for a three year term. If the *gromada* is poor, the office carries no salary but is purely honorary. And the honour is slight in comparison to the demands of the position. Some duties of the *Soltys* are: to help administer the Federal tax system, to issue certificates, passports, etc., to lead the members of the *gromada* when they are needed for road building.

These are not tasks that make a man popular, and there are few candidates for the job—rather, men try to avoid it. The usual tendency is to select as *Soltys* a man who is neither very rich nor very poor.

The next larger administrative unit is the *gmina*, headed by a *Voyt*, who presides over it at meetings. The *gmina* is a representative body made up of selected delegates from several *gromady*. Its officers, in addition to the *Voyt*, are two assistants and a number of aldermen—twelve, in *gminy* of five thousand or under, a larger number if the membership is over five thousand.

The position of *Voyt* is far more important, far more lucrative, and far more sought after than that of *Soltys*. Interest in the elections is keen and at times excitement runs high. Usually a comparatively rich man is elected, but he will always be a man of the people.

In the past, the *Voyt's* symbol of office was his official rod, which was sent about from house to house when he wanted to call a meeting. The cane was an elaborately carved staff, which belonged to the office itself and not to the current incumbent. This is no longer used.

Several *gminy* are combined into a district, headed by a *Starosta*. The *Starosta* is not elected like the *Soltys* and the *Voyt*, but is appointed by the national administration. He is not, like the other officials, one of the group he governs, but comes from the other side of the social chasm that separates peasants from the upper classes. Final decision on many questions reviewed by the *gmina* rests with him.

He has final decision also on the election of the *Voyt*, who must be approved by the *Starosta* before he becomes an official functionary. If he is not approved, a new election must be held.

It is very important to the peasants to have the *Voyt* they want, and they do not easily submit to a veto by the *Starosta*. They may stubbornly elect the same *Voyt* all over again, and there may be as many as three elections before agreement is reached. Such refusal to bow to the *Starosta's* will may be on principle as well as for practical reasons, for the peasant is jealous of his independence. Characteristically he submits to tyrannies sanctioned by tradition, and fiercely resists any violation of his traditional rights.

The long history of feudalism is both a background to and a present factor in the pattern of Polish life, especially for the peasants, who represent over two-thirds of the total population. For three hundred years, until 1784, the peasants were serfs, bound to their land and to their lords. After that, although the Constitution of 1791 nominally changed their status, there was little real change in their position or condition until Poland was reconstituted in 1919, after the first World War.

The mark of feudalism is evident in the Polish class structure, with its large proportion of peasants and small minority of nobility, or *szlachta*. For a long period the middle-class was negligible, and until 1939 it was extremely small, while the Polish intelligentsia were functionally an extension of the nobility, with much the same outlook. The working-class, also a comparatively new group, has been functionally an extension of the peasant class. Its members have been recruited from landless peasants or those with very small holdings, from handicraft workers who found themselves unable to compete with modern factories, and to a small extent, from abroad. Before World War II, industrial wage earners made up twenty-nine per cent of the population. Only the skilled workers, who were unionized, received adequate wages.

The ties between peasants and city workers have been very close. During periods of unemployment, workers have returned to their native villages and in winter, when farm work is slack, the sons of peasant families have gone to the cities to work for short periods.

The struggle to wrest a living from farmland inadequate in size and often not particularly fertile is the basic cause of the extreme poverty of the peasants, which is proverbial throughout Europe. The average cash income of the Polish peasant in 1934-35 was exactly two cents or less than twopence a day, according to the Polish Ministry of Finance. Lack of money forced them to sell their produce as soon as it was harvested, regardless of the price obtained—and often regardless of their own diet. At times it forced them to eat grain reserved for next year's planting, a necessity tragic for any farmer.

The feudal tradition has been visible too in the land distribution, until the effective breaking up of estates began in 1946. Before that, about sixty per cent of all farms were too small to support a family, while at the same time almost half of the arable land was owned by a landed nobility representing less than six-tenths of one per cent of the agricultural population. Medium-sized farms have played a very limited role in Poland. The great majority of peasants—almost ten million —owned farms too small to furnish a family subsistence. The situation was aggravated by further division of the land into separate holdings, according to the traditional inheritance custom, and by the three-field system.

The hangover of feudalism is apparent too in peasant attitudes toward each other, toward other social groups, and toward life. Yet in Poland the pattern of feudalism has received a special colouring from the Polish conception of individual independence and liberty. Distance between social classes has been accepted and observed. Within each class, however, there is almost fanatical insistence on the equality of individuals. The pre-eminence of one man over his social peers is resented, if it is tolerated at all.

The special concept of liberty and equality, as held by the nobility, has been a dominant influence in shaping Polish history. Among the peasants it has been a leading motif in shaping basic attitudes. That it is recognized by outsiders is evident in generalizations made about the Poles: 'Every Pole is an exception to every rule,' they say; or 'a Pole would rather bow to a foreigner than give authority to one of his own group.'

The social cleavage between peasants and *szlachta* was absolute, and unbridgeable. Yet along with acceptance of social inferiority, the peasant maintains a stubborn self-respect. He knows what is correct, and he knows his own rights. Though he may be overborne in fact, he will not yield in principle.

His rights require that no outsider shall invade his private affairs or his private domain. When the government insisted that each man in a village must paint his fence, there was trouble. Not only does paint cost money, but a man's yard is his own, to do with as he likes. If a *Voyt* comes to see a peasant on official business, he will ask very politely for permission to enter his house. If he failed to do so he would forfeit support and respect; for a man's home is his own, and inviolable.

The counterpart of insistence on his own rights is the peasant's recognition of the rights of others. To each his own—his own rights and privileges, his own place, his own customs. Let him have them—and let him respect mine!

Toward city people the peasant maintains an attitude of aloofness untainted by admiration. He may envy what he feels to be their easy life and easy money, but he admits no desire to become one of them. His own ways are the ones he respects, likes, clings to; his own land is the focus of his ambition.

According to the peasant, every city is a welter of corruption. 'City people are without God. They lie and undermine you, and there is no sincerity. They don't regard the peasant as a man; they look down on him and suppress him. They don't believe in God and they have no fear of Hell. Terrible people!'

There is no limit, he feels, to the arrogance of the city dweller, the *pan*. They will all stand together against a humble farmer. When a peasant has an argument with a *pan* he usually prefers to give in and reach some compromise because, as he says, 'A dog is not going to bite another dog's tail.' Or, 'the bottom of the truth fell out long ago.' So the peasant sits quiet, feeling helpless before the *pan*.

That the *pan* does in fact regard the peasant as an inferior being is clearly evident. It is suggested by the avoidance of the word for peasant when a *pan* wants to be polite. Instead of using the word *chlop*—which literally means merely male— he will refer to the peasant as a 'village dweller'. Daughters of country gentry have been reduced to tears by the mere

CYCLE OF THE SEASONS   37

coloured by Christian elements, wholly conforming to the elaborate ritual and religious flavour of the Church, the majority of Polish holidays have as their basis agricultural rites first celebrated by the ancients, perhaps the aboriginal people of Poland. In adopting Christianity the peasant did not give up the customs and habits of pre-Christian times. The pagan divinities to whom he paid homage, and whose services he invoked at certain seasons of the year, remained with him; and only gradually their attributes were transferred to the Christian saints.

This transference was made with the acquiescence and often with the deliberate encouragement of the Church, providing the pagan practices did not conflict with religious tenets. Practices savouring of black magic and ancestor worship were frowned upon, however, and were dis-couraged—not always with success.

Whatever their origin, the colourful, varied festivities are felt to contribute to the fertility, the prosperity, the safety of fields, farm animals, and the farm folk themselves. They serve both as insurance of success and as omens of what may be expected. Even when full belief in them has waned, a suspicion has crept in that it is best to be on the safe side.

When exiles or emigrants are homesick for Poland they are likely to think first of these gala occasions. The author's most appreciated articles about Poland have been descriptions of holidays and festivals. Exiles would like to do the same things in their new homes. Even second generation emigrants, who have never been part of that life, want to learn about—and often to observe—the holiday customs.

There is much for the exile to remember. Few peasants have more holidays than the Poles, and probably few need more. The poverty, toil, and stern restraints of the regular routine demand socially sanctioned explosions of colour, gaiety, and occasionally of violence. When music and dancing are unrestrained and vodka or mead flow freely, brawls are not uncommon.

Most of the holidays are related to, and named for, some saint. As in all Christendom, practically every day of the year carries the name of a saint, the special patron of that day, and is referred to merely by his name. February 14, for example, will be called 'St. Valentine's' rather than 'St. Valentine's Day'.

In Poland, due partly to piety but also because printed calendars are a rarity in peasant homes, the peasant literally marks his year, measures his time, plans his work, indeed guides his life by the days of the saints. Countless proverbs, rhymed to the saint's name, tell the farmer when to start sowing, when to begin the harvest, which days are appropriate for certain tasks and which days are bad.

The saints are important personages, and an important part of daily life. To the peasant, the heavenly host is a large family, much like his own here on earth. There is a fixed hierarchy within which these supernatural beings have been assigned specific tasks related to his everyday pattern of living. Respect, affection and awe mingle with the practical consideration of what they can do for him.

While the peasant knows from his catechism that there is but one God, who dominates the Holy Trinity, this concept is rather vague to him. He is essentially a practical man, with little bent for mysticism and little interest in religious dogma. Christ, the Virgin Mary and the saints are intimate, familiar figures who function in his daily life as counsellors, protectors, and helpers. The holy pictures that adorn every peasant home are regarded not only as charms against misfortune, but also as portraits of real individuals.

The saints possess distinct personalities and decidedly human traits. Although in principle there exists a tie of solidarity and cooperation among them, they may quarrel, be jealous, compete with or trick each other. By the same token they may take offence if they are not sufficiently honoured, for they are sensitive to attention and to the lack of it. One may argue and bargain with the saints, or even threaten them, for they are subject to human emotions and motives.

Although each saint has prescribed duties, their functions may overlap. The same anecdote may even be told about two different saints in different places. And although they play endless tricks on each other, for the most part these are practical jokes, not really 'mean'. If one saint shirks his duty, another may step in and help. Or if two saints seem hopelessly at odds, the peasant may appeal to the boundless sympathy of the Holy Mother.

There are countless tales and legends illustrating the peasant's attitude toward the saints. While religious dogmas are never discussed except in church, droll stories about the saints are a favourite pastime in the field, the home or the village inn.

There are lesser and greater saints, depending upon the position they had held in the world before their deaths, their status with God, the weight of their assignment, or the innate force of their personalities. Moreover, although the whole activity of God and the saints is bound to the supernatural, it is a fixed activity and cannot break the normal order of things. Because of its stability, this activity lies within the realm of prediction for the peasant. The Holy Mother alone performs miracles and these are always beneficial to the people.

Regardless of help or favour from the heavenly family, the farmer must do his share: one must work in order to achieve. Of course there is always the possibility that a man's best efforts will be frustrated by the negligence of a saint or by evil forces. Disasters on the farm are often ascribed to the carelessness, frivolity or momentary incapacity of the saints, or perhaps even to a misunderstanding or quarrel among them.

The degree of veneration which the peasant accords to the various saints does not depend so much on their relative sanctity as upon the seriousness of the havoc their anger could cause in his affairs. Veneration is displayed by the correct placing and decorating of the saint's picture, and in some places, the lighting of a candle before it on the proper occasions, the observance of the correct ritual at the prescribed moment. Such veneration is largely prompted by fear of revenge on the part of a slighted or neglected saint, and of God's added punishment meted out to one who has dared to show a lack of respect for any of His Servants.

Each man, each community, each occupation, each season, each illness or crisis has a special patron saint. In short, it is a firm belief of the peasant that there is hardly a situation where one cannot help himself through a prayer addressed to the proper saint.

Magical practices are applied in order to reinforce the potency of religious ceremonies and to counteract the workings of evil spirits, among whom devils and witches are conspicuous and active. Such magic is strictly practical in purpose. For the peasant, however, there is no clear-cut distinction between magical and religious observances. They are merged in one supernatural, which itself is not sharply divorced from the workings of the natural world.

Some magical practices are known only to the initiate; others are practised by everybody, often as part of the holiday celebrations. There is a distinction between those experts who use magic for worthy purposes and those who use it to harm others—that is, who indulge in black magic. The harmful group includes magicians and witches, male and female. The benevolent group includes medicine-women and fortune-tellers. Even the benevolent magicians are feared, because of their power. As for those who indulge in black magic, they are regarded with fright and hostility. It is not difficult for an individual, especially one who is old, to incur suspicion of practising witchcraft, and it is a real misfortune for a villager to be so suspected.

A commonly dreaded kind of black magic is that which takes the milk away from the cow. It is practised by a female witch and the procedure is as follows: early in the morning, before sunrise, the witch takes a rag used in milking and gathers into it dew from the grass, saying as she does so, 'Now I am taking the milk away from the cow.' This will cause the cow to go dry.

Such a witch may get her power either by being born with it, or by selling her soul and body to the Devil. The sale would be made by calling upon the Devil late at night, saying, 'Devil, take my body and soul, but give me milk.' The Devil himself does not teach the novice the tricks of her trade, but sends her to a woman wise in magical practices.

The power of the evil eye—spoken of as 'evil eyes'—is commanded not only by magicians and witches, but by anyone who is considered to be bad. People are also suspected of possessing this power if their eyes have any unusual characteristic—if they are inflamed and red, or unusually piercing. It is believed that anyone, who as a child was permitted to feed at the breast again after the sudden weaning period, customary in Poland, would develop 'evil eyes'.

Animals as well as humans may have the power of the evil eye, but with animals it is usually exercised through some part of the anatomy other than the eye. For example, it is thought that the peacock may exert it through the 'eyes' of his tail.

Those most susceptible to harm through the evil eye are domestic animals, children, pregnant women, and people about to embark on some happy enterprise such as marriage.

The effects of the evil eye are illness, loss of property, damage to property, and general bad luck.

The Devil, who entered Poland with Christianity, is an object of humour rather than of fear. A great mass of legends and beliefs, attributed in olden times to various pagan gods and demons, were later transferred to him. The usual assumption is that there is a chief devil and many lesser ones of varying power and shrewdness. Their origin is explained in numerous tales relating to the revolt of the bad angels and their expulsion from heaven.

The Devil is very often cited in proverbs and anecdotes, tales and stories, and in cursing. He is pictured in many different ways, but always as exotic and never resembling a peasant. He can change himself into any animal except a pigeon or a stork. Most of the time he is invisible, but there are ways to detect his presence. And although most devils are very sly, a clever peasant knows how to deal with him, and can even fool him as is clear in countless tales.

The Devil said to a peasant, 'I will give you a barrel full of gold if you will give me your head.' The peasant said, 'All right. Bring this barrel of gold and come back to my garden for the head.' The Devil brought the barrel of gold, and came to the garden. And the peasant showed him cabbage heads and told him, 'Take one.' But the Devil said, 'I don't want the cabbage heads; I want your head!' So the peasant said: 'I haven't got a head; I've only got a noodle.' And he added, 'If you don't believe it, we will go to the inn, and we'll ask everybody about it.'

At the inn, the peasant asked a man who was drunk, 'Hey, tell me what is this?' and showed him the head of the cabbage. The drunkard said: 'What a stupid question! That's the head of a cabbage!' And then the peasant showed him his own head and asked, 'Is that a head?' And the drunkard said, 'No, you haven't got a head; you only have a noodle!' So the peasant asked the Devil, 'Did you hear that?' And so as to convince him even better, he started an argument with the innkeeper. The innkeeper said to him: 'If you don't stop this, I'll cut off your noodle.' So the peasant said to the Devil: 'Well, you see—go your way.' And the Devil left, and the gold stayed with the peasant.

Devils are sometimes grateful for good treatment, and hence the proverb, 'A candle for God and for the Devil the stub of a candle.'

Devils and other evil spirits are particularly active on the strips of grass, called *miedza*, which mark the boundary lines between the cultivated fields. All kinds of bad magic may occur on these uncultivated borders which belong to nobody except the evil spirits. A popular folk tale, for example, tells of a man who carelessly left his lunch on the *miedza* where it was captured by a mischievous little devil. Crossroads are another favourite haunt of devils and bogies, even though such spots are often presided over by roadside shrines.

It would be impossible to describe all the holidays in which the diverse yet strongly welded elements of peasant belief are dramatized. A description of the chief ones, however, will give a picture of the variety and colour the Polish festivals display, and also of the basic themes and practices that run through many of them.

SPRING

Though snow is falling
It will not destroy the tree
Though snow is floating
It will not harm our tree
The snow winds about the fence
But the peas will come up in the garden
The snow is falling on the meadow
But the grain will come up slowly.

The farmer's year begins with spring. After the long ordeal of winter with its darkness, its tedium and its cold, life seems to be born again. All is activity, and all activity is geared toward the new crops.

This is the season of the first sowing in the field, the first planting in the garden; the season when cattle and sheep are taken out to pasture and when other important tasks are completed about the farm and stockyard.

The first sowing is usually carried out with devout ceremony. In former times, and frequently today, the Polish farmer would dress for the occasion in holiday attire. The family gathers for prayers before he sets out, often joined by the priest who comes to offer his special blessing over all.

With the seed bag about his neck, the sower walks slowly along the furrows in dignified concentration. He scatters the seed in a sweeping movement, like a priest bestowing benediction. The sowing is done in complete silence, usually by the farmer himself as he cannot trust this ceremonious duty to hired or less experienced hands. This was not always so. In former times both the sowing of grain and the planting of fruit were assigned to the young in keeping with the proverb, 'things will not grow after an old man'.

Spring lays the foundation for the farmer's year. When it is over he says, 'We've done the spring work' rejoicing that the year's hardest toil is behind him. But even though it is the most strenuous of the seasons, it is also the best loved.

All the holidays of springtime centre around the theme of resurrection, the symbol of life conquering cold death. Easter, the most important holiday of this most important season, is also the most important holiday of the whole year. Its ceremonies are longer, more solemn and more elaborate even than those of Christmas. Throughout the land, in cities as well as in the rural areas, no holiday is more eagerly awaited, none celebrated more joyously or with richer pageantry.

The long stretch of Easter holidays begins with Shrovetide and ends after Holy Week. Interwoven with the religious ritual and celebration, and extending beyond the limits of the Easter holidays proper, runs the dramatization and celebration of winter's death and spring's return. It is all one theme and all felt as part of one order, whether spring is welcomed as a beautiful maiden, symbolized by a green branch, or

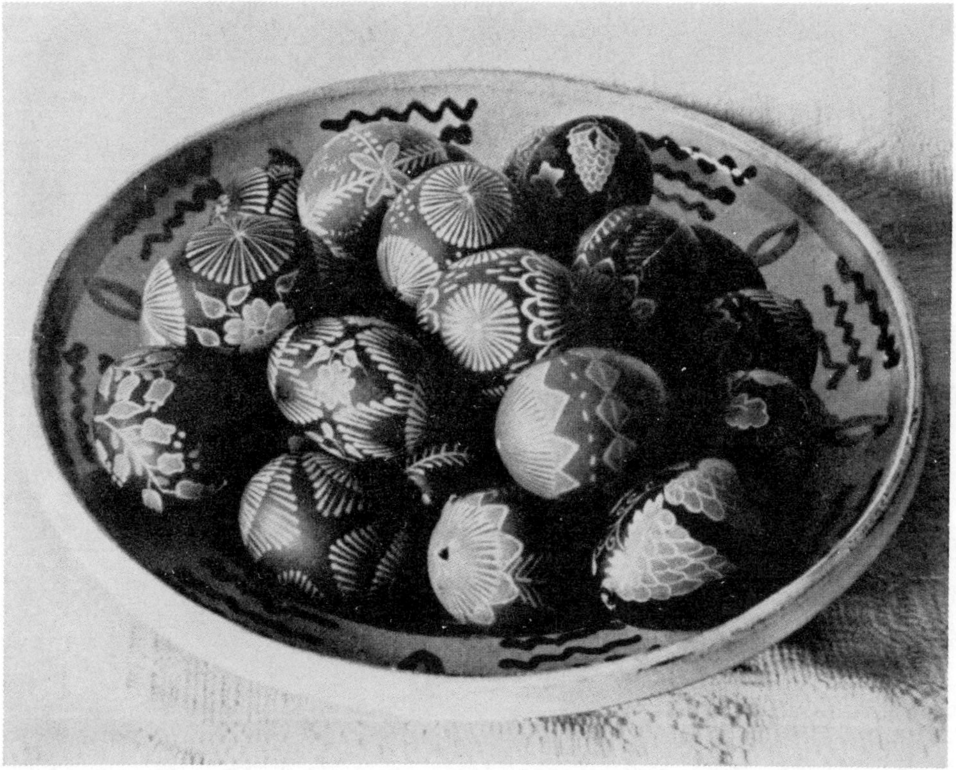

COLOURED EGGS FOR EASTER

'FLIGHT TO EGYPT'—WOOD SCULPTURE

appreciated as the protégé and gift of St. George; whether the rejoicing takes the form of Christian ritual or of rites handed down from forgotten pagan sources.

The final days before Lent are known as *Tlustne dni*, the fat days, in contrast to the lean meatless ones that will follow. Sometimes they are called *Ostatki*, the remaining days; or *Zapusty*, the empty days. The Shrovetide festivities during *Zapusty* are a carnival period, and as the carnival approaches its climax the whole village becomes the scene of gay parades in which many masks appear, both animal and human. The animals most commonly represented are the horse, the goat, and the rooster. The human figures, dubbed Karnawal, Death, and Marzanna, are thought of as symbolizing winter. Marzanna was, in fact, the name of the ancient pagan goddess of Death.

The passing of winter is dramatized by carrying out of the village and destroying—usually 'drowning'—the straw image of Marzanna, a ceremony which may take place at various other times, from Shrovetide to the fourth Sunday of Lent.

The Shrovetide paraders wind their way through the village streets, dressed in fantastic and elaborate costumes, with their masks of straw, leather, wood or rags. The agrarian magic behind their gay antics is revealed in a song commonly sung as they march:

> *Make merry, little horse*
> *In the green grove*
> *Where our horse walks*
> *There grain will grow.*

After singing their songs, the masqueraders give the usual 'Praise the Lord!' and perform their repertory of tricks, for which they receive small gifts of money. The collection is put into a common fund to be used for a final flourish in the village tavern.

The theme of human fertility is also prominent during the

D

Shrovetide carnival. Marriageable young men and women who failed to choose a mate during the preceding season are penalized on this day. Chicken feet, turkey wind-pipes, herring skeletons, or other unattractive objects are pinned on them as, dressed in their best, they enter the church. Verses are often pinned on them too, like the following:

> *If, gracious maiden, you walked in a pair*
> *You would not now carry this block of wood—*
> *In penance for your spinsterhood*
> *Bear as your badge this turkey foot.*

Another practice, the privilege of the older married women, is that of tying logs or blocks of wood to the unmated. This ceremony is carried off with much noise and fanfare. The unfortunates must pay a ransom, the collective sum being used for drinks bought in the tavern at the climax of the proceedings.

In some regions of Poland the old men used to lie in wait throughout the village for single men who should have married during the preceding season, capture them unawares, then chain them to huge logs which the bachelors had to pull about. A man could buy his way out of the indignity by standing drinks for all at the village tavern.

This practice has fallen into disuse in recent years. Its substitute survives, however, in the form of token logs which are pinned on both young women and men, along with the ignominious herring bone and turkey-foot, as they enter the church.

A high spot of the festivity is the auctioning of the girls— another link between *Zapusty* and the ancient rites of courting couples in the spring. Toward evening the young men herd the young women into a hut or tavern, and there jokingly bargain for them after the fashion of cattle-dealing at the fairs. When a young man chooses a girl for whom he will bargain, she retires with him to a manger filled with hay, where he closely examines her teeth, nose, and other features. If she meets with his approval they finally seal the bargain between themselves, after many humorous exchanges and bickerings. Then they return to the tavern, where the purchaser hands the master of ceremonies a few pennies in payment for his partner. The 'bartered' girl will reward the youth who 'bought' her with a gift of coloured eggs when Easter arrives. If a girl is so unfortunate as not to find a purchaser, she is put out-of-doors in disgrace.

Married women come into their own during the Shrovetide festivities. Not only do they chastise the unmated, but they force the brides of the season to buy their way into the charmed circle of established matrons. The practice is called 'buying into the married women'. In one region of Poland on the Eve of Ash Wednesday—that is, on Shrove Tuesday— the married women, dressed in men's hats and overcoats, gather all the new brides and take them to the tavern in sleighs. There the young brides pay a ransom which gives them entree into the society of matrons, and at the same time provides refreshments with which to celebrate their new status.

Another Shrove Tuesday dance of the married women originally was designed to make the hemp grow tall. The women gather in the tavern and when they begin to feel the liquor they dance around a barrel on which stands a *koziolek,* or 'little ram'—a small figure made of wood and pieces of cloth. During the dance they try to leap as high as possible, to make the hemp grow high. The men spur them on, as each woman tries to outdo the others, and the serious purpose of the dance is buried under waves of merriment.

Shrove Tuesday with its dancing and gaiety officially closes the carnival season. Huge quantities of doughnuts are consumed on that day, in anticipation of Lent when they will be taboo.

Ash Wednesday ushers in Lent. Singing and amusements cease as all take to darker, more sombre dress, the girls shedding beads, ribbons and other ornaments. Meat and all the more palatable dishes are abandoned. The two chief foods of the farmer and his family through Lent will be herring and *zur*, a gruel made from fermented rye meal and water.

In the churches, the ceremony of Ash Wednesday reaches a climax when the priest sprinkles ashes on the heads of the worshippers.

Prefaced by the long six weeks of Lent, the climax of the Easter season begins with Palm Sunday, known in Poland as Flower Sunday. Everyone goes to church on that day, bearing 'palms' to be blessed by the priest during the service. The 'palms' are usually long sprigs of pussy-willow that were cut during the first week of Lent and kept in water indoors, so that they would produce catkins in time for the eventful day. Swallowing the blessed catkins is believed to give protection against sore throat.

The 'palm' may be pine branches or branches of other forest evergreens. In recent times in the cities and occasionally in the villages, true palms may be imported from abroad. The consecrated 'palms' are thought to have protective properties and are kept through the year. They are thrust behind pictures of the saints or put on window sills as a barrier against lightning. In certain areas it is believed that if fronds of the blessed 'palm' are stuck into the entrances of mole hills on Easter Sunday, they will drive these pests away and prevent them from damaging the crops.

Flogging on Palm Sunday is almost universal throughout Poland. Few escape the switch at some time during the day except the very old, and even they receive a token flogging. Children and young people are the chief victims, however, since the young are symbolic of the crops and flogging is thought to induce health and growth.

The first one up on Palm Sunday morning will waken the others with a lash of the switch, shouting good-humouredly as he strikes:

The willow smites, but does not kill—
The great day is but a week away—
And cuts the flesh but once a year.

Flogging may take place on other days also, as in Pomerania where on Maundy Thursday the housewife beats each member of her family with a gooseberry twig until he cries in memory of the crown of thorns. Known as *Boze rany*, or God's wounds, the custom is explained as representing the penance of Christ on the cross. The beating of man and crops to induce good growth is also found in ancient pagan ritual, and is practised also in conjunction with the Christmas holidays and Ash Wednesday.

In some places Palm Sunday is marked by processions with a donkey, in commemoration of Christ's entry into Jerusalem. Also, in some areas this day rather than St. George's is the one for driving the cattle from their winter quarters into the pastures.

The entire week between Palm Sunday and Easter is devoted to praying, attending church, and above all to preparing for the great day. The cottage is thoroughly swept, scrubbed and put in order. Walls and ceilings are whitewashed, the wooden furniture is scrubbed and polished, and the room is decorated with potted plants and with artificial flowers, cut out of coloured paper with infinite patience and ingenuity.

All this the women do, while the men make order about the courtyards, stables and barns, and bring up reserves of fodder and grain in order to have more leisure for the holidays. If the household economy permits the slaughtering of a pig, the whole family works at cutting and boning, making sausages and hams. In the course of the week, gifts of meat and sausage will be taken to neighbours and poor relations, each receiving the correct portion, according to elaborate and rigid rules.

Farm work is not entirely neglected during Holy Week, and certain tasks are definitely prescribed. Holy Tuesday and, in some areas, Good Friday are regarded as particularly good days for planting peas and potatoes. This is done no matter what the weather, nor how great the pressure of other tasks, because the success of the crop depends on its favourable auspices.

One of the chief occupations of the week is preparing food for *Swiecone*, the blessing of the Easter fare. Bread and cake made from wheat flour and yeast are in every oven, and appetizing smells of baking and roasting flow through the village.

During Holy Week are prepared also the coloured eggs which to the people are chief symbols of Easter, and the outstanding feature of the Easter feast. The practice of decorating Easter eggs, is known throughout the entire Christian world, but has been developed into an elaborate and complex art in Poland and Ruthenia. In Poland the development has been long, reaching back to the eleventh century and before.

Men have no part in decorating the Easter eggs. This is traditionally the work of girls, though young married women may help if they can spare time from their many other tasks. The decorating is made a social occasion. Girls gather together and work for the entire evening, in friendly competition for the most novel and delightful effects.

To produce the decorated eggs, or *pisanki*, requires patience, skill, and considerable technical knowledge. Wax is applied by means of a needle or a tiny metal tube (usually the tip of a shoe lace) set in a small piece of wood. The parts coated with wax will not take the colour when the egg is dipped.

To achieve multi-coloured effects, the egg is waxed and dipped repeatedly; then the wax is removed and a new pattern applied. There are many secrets about design and colour—what combinations of lines and forms will give an exquisite effect, what bark or berry the desired colour. For example, to get the most delicate light green, one should use moss and be sure to take it from under a stone. Orange can be made from an infusion of crocuses, and black is brewed from alder bark or cones, or from young leaves of the black plane-tree.

The designs fall in to three general categories: geometric patterns, stylized representations of household furniture and tools, and motifs from plant and animal life. These designs are numerous and have definite names such as 'the mill', 'the pine tree', 'the dove'. As in all Polish folk art, there is great scope for individuality and variation within fixed limits. While traditional motifs are observed, each decorator may elaborate them freely 'out of the head' as the Polish phrase goes.

The colours and designs employed, and the mastery of execution, vary from area to area. The most beautiful and elaborate *pisanki* of the mountain region, for instance, would rank with the finest batik production of the Orient. It is remarkable that so much painstaking labour, so much inventiveness and skill should be lavished on something as fragile as an eggshell.

These eggs, however, are often treated as works of art, at least *pro tem*. They are put on display in the home, and perhaps kept for a long time. They are presented as gifts, to godparents and to friends. A gift of an Easter egg from a girl to a young man is a sign that his attentions will not be unwelcome. Easter eggs are not presented to one's own parents or children, for the pattern of Polish family life does not encourage such exchange of gifts.

Progressing parallel to the secular preparations and

festivities, the church observances of Holy Week differ little
from those in Catholic churches throughout the world.
There are masses in the morning and Stations of the Cross—
Gorzkie Żale—Bitter Sorrows—in the afternoons. The traditional Christian rite of washing the feet on Maundy Thursday
was known in former times but seems now to have vanished
from the practices surrounding Holy Week.

This week is considered a lucky time for a person to die,
not only because of its exalted mood and constant church
attendance. All the graves are open then and 'the earth will
lie lightly upon him', he will rest in peace.

At noon on Thursday, the church bell and the organ are
stilled. From then until the bells peal out for the Resurrection, the church is hushed in silent prayer, in contemplation
of the pain of Christ, in wrapt work over the Holy sepulchre
that is being made ready for Easter morning.

Good Friday is a solemn day. Fasting is rigorous, often to
the point of complete abstention even from bread and water.

On Holy Saturday the religious tension and solemnity
relax somewhat. This is a day of consecration, in preparation
for Easter Sunday and the new year it ushers in. The morning is devoted to the ceremony of consecrating fire and water.
The fire on the hearth is extinguished and some member of
the household—usually the housewife—goes to church to
light a candle from the flame of a church candle that has been
blessed by a priest. She brings home the lighted candle, and
with in a bottle of holy water, also blessed during the church
services. She guards the flame of the candle carefully as she
makes her way home, and with it relights the fire on the
hearth.

The ceremony furnishes the occasion for cleaning the
hearth of the grime and rubbish accumulated during the
winter, but this utilitarian purpose is veiled by the religious
and magical significance of the new light. The 'eternal lamp'

which burns in almost every home before the picture of the Holy Virgin is also put out and relighted immediately from the flame of the blessed candle.

A sip of the consecrated water is given to each member of the family, to ward off sore throat. Then the livestock are sprinkled with it, so that they will bear easily. Finally the trees in the orchard are sprinkled, to insure a good crop.

In some localities the sprinkling is done on Easter Sunday, when the family returns from church. Either the head of the household or the first person back from Mass takes the palm blessed on Palm Sunday and, using it as an aspergillum, sprinkles all the members of the household, the animals, and the buildings with the holy water.

A gay ceremony of Holy Saturday is the burning of the *zur* and the herring (where herring is available) which were the chief fare during Lent, and which are heartily despised by the end of the six-week period. The youth of the village take a pot of *zur* and add to it various nauseous objects. With mock solemnity, to the accompaniment of music, the beat of drums, and noisy cries of '*Zur, zur, wynos sie*'—'*Zur, zur,* get thee gone!'—they carry the offensive gruel out of the village and bury it.

The herring, sometimes a real one but more often a carved wooden effigy, is tied to a string and dragged ignominiously through the village to a burial place. Formerly this burial might be graced by a formal oration addressed to the late, unlamented fish. 'Herring, herring, thou wilt not starve our stomachs any longer, for we will trounce thee and hang thee on a tree.' Post-Lenten revenge on the herring in one form or another is practised throughout the land, in cities and country alike.

The most important business of Holy Saturday, however, is the blessing of the food, *Swiecone*. To this, all the activities of the week have been directed. The house has been cleaned and freshly decorated. Sprigs of green have been brought from the woods, to deck the walls and table, to be stuck into the ham or butter, or to edge the platters of sausage and cake. The table is laid with the housewife's finest linen, displaying the wealth of the cottage on 'the great day'. Hams, pig's head, roast veal, pig's trotter jelly, sausages of various kinds wound in huge coils on separate plates or in a ring around the ham, cakes of all kinds—particularly the mound-shaped *baba*, eggs—some shelled and some decorated, are spread in profusion on the table.

In the centre is placed the Paschal lamb, made of butter by the organist or his wife, or by nuns if there is a convent near by, or else by a gifted member of the family. Grated horse-radish in vinegar, alone or mixed with grated beetroot, is always on the table. In some localities a little of the horse-radish mixture is taken as the very first mouthful of the Easter feast, in commemoration of Christ's bitter cup of gall.

If the household is a prosperous one, the priest comes in person to bless the food. This is a great honour and a source of deep satisfaction. Less opulent families take their food to the house of a wealthier neighbour who has a room large enough to hold additional tables, so that the priest can bless the food of several families at once. In cities and larger towns, where the parishes are very large, the food is brought to church in baskets and blessed there. If even this is impossible, either because of distance, illness in the family, or poverty, someone takes salt, oil and vinegar to be blessed in symbolic representation of the whole feast.

No matter what hardships surround the problem of having the food blessed, to be without sanctified food on Easter day is unthinkable. Where the inhabitants of a village have no church and are miles away from the nearest one—distances often impassable at Easter-time because of spring thaws and flood-destroyed bridges—a special emissary is sent out, carrying a small but representative sample of food to be blessed at the nearest church. If the spring floods make any sort of communication impossible, the Easter fare is sanctified by being sprinkled with salt that was blessed the previous year.

The belief is common that water acquires healing properties on Holy Saturday. People go to streams and ponds and wash their wounds so that they may heal faster. If one bathes in the waters before sunrise, he will not only haste the healing of wounds but will also be protected against skin diseases during the coming year.

Easter day opens with the Resurrection Mass. In many churches the service begins late Saturday evening and lasts until daybreak on Sunday. In most, however, it is held at dawn on Easter morning. Dressed in their best clothes, tense with hope and the significance of the hour, old and young hasten to the holiest service of the year.

Formerly the young men and boys celebrated by firing guns for several hours before church time. They shot neither at game nor at targets, the purpose being merely to make noise and mark the occasion as unusual. Because many accidents resulted, the authorities have forbidden this practice in recent years, much to the chagrin of the young people for whom shooting is a favourite pastime.

After services, people start for home eagerly, racing to get there first. For the man who is first to return home from the services will be first to harvest his crops. Moreover, the first one home wins the honour of sprinkling family, house, and live-stock with holy water.

Soon after returning from church the family gather to eat the elaborately prepared, sanctified food. According to time-honoured tradition, the Easter feast begins with the sharing of a blessed egg by the entire family. An egg is cut into as many pieces as there are persons present, and a few extra ones for guests who may drop in. Each person takes a piece of the diced egg from the plate as it is passed by the household head or another important member. Blessings for long life and happiness are exchanged as the bits of egg are eaten.

After the egg has been shared by all present, and solemn and hopeful wishes have been voiced, the family sit down to their festive meal. All eat silently, savouring the food after their long fast, but careful to avoid any show of eagerness or greed. With restraint and decorum they express appreciation of the feast. After the first intense hunger is satisfied and the free-flowing mead or vodka has been enjoyed, the solemn and polite mood relaxes and tongues loosen. The rest of the day will be given over to the holiday spirit.

Great magical potency is attributed to the blessed food, and none of it must be wasted or profaned by irreverent treatment. Bones from the meats are thrown into the well to keep worms from breeding in the water; crumbs from the table are carefully gathered and thrown into the garden; egg-shells are hung on fruit trees to improve the crop.

By-products from the preparation of the food are also believed to have magic powers. For example, the fat may be skimmed from the top of the pot in which the ham is boiled, and carefully put away. When the farmer goes out to sow millet he will smear his hands with this fat, in order to keep the sparrows from eating the seed. In one region, people save the shells from the eggs used at the Easter table and scatter them in nooks and crannies of the cottage to keep out vermin and frogs. Even the water in which the eggs were boiled finds a use: it is poured on the threshold of the cow-shed, where it will ward off the witches who would otherwise come to steal the milk.

Easter Monday is known in Poland as *Dyngus*, *Śmigus*, or *Święty Lej*. The name *Dyngus* comes from the German *Dingnis*, meaning ransom—it is possible to buy immunity from the punishment to which the day is dedicated. The punishment is called *oblewanki*, or drenching with water. This man-made downpour is supposed to evoke the rains so greatly needed for spring sowing. In theory, on Monday the boys douse the girls while the girls avenge themselves on Tuesday. In actual practice, Monday is the day for both sexes, since the girls do not take their punishment passively. Activities begin at daybreak. Armed with bottles, buckets or any vessel that will hold water, the boys break into the girls' homes, take them by surprise while they are still in bed, and drench them thoroughly 'for health and good harvests'.

The more intelligent girls build barricades on the night before *Dyngus,* but these are usually ineffective, as the boys will brook no obstacles. The *Dyngus* may take violent form; girls are sometimes carried out, bed and all, and ducked in a pond or nearby river. In general, however, the ceremonies do not exceed the limits of rough but good-natured play.

There also exists a refined form of the *Dyngus*. Among peasants who have risen in the social scale and acquired 'genteel' manners, and among city folk, the dousing is replaced by sprinkling, sometimes with water but more often with perfume or cologne.

In former times, a young man would mount the roof of the village tavern, beat loudly on a tin pan, and call out the names of the girls who were to be doused. As he called each name he would specify how many wagon loads of sand, how much water and how much soap would be used on each girl. There was a versified formula for answering this roof-top taunt, to the effect that the girl was not afraid for there was someone who would save her. From the tavern roof would come the announcement that Zoska, because she dressed badly, kept her house untidily, and quarrelled with everyone, will have a *Dyngus* of a hundred barrels of water, a hundred cartloads of sand and a hundred lashes. Then from a window would come the reply that Zoska is not frightened for Jasiek stands beside her with a bottle of whiskey to buy off all assailants and ransom her from the penalty.

The *Dyngus* processions begin on Monday in some areas, but more often on Tuesday morning. The younger boys go through the village in a noisy march known as *chodzenie po dyngusie*—'going on the *Dyngus*', or *z kogutkiem*—'with the cockerel'. A cock is put on a small, two-wheeled wagon which has been painted red and decorated with bright ribbons and artificial flowers. Often the little cart also carries small puppets representing a wedding party.

In some places the boys spot the handsomest cock in the village and capture him for temporary use, without the owner's leave. On the eve of *Dyngus* they give him vodka or feed him grain soaked in alcohol, allegedly to make him sit quiet and crow loudly on the morrow. A cock carved out of wood, at times ingeniously contrived, and perhaps decorated with real cock's feathers, is often used as a substitute.

Crowing like roosters and singing religious and comic songs, the boys proceed from cottage to cottage. They try to please and amuse every household in order to receive from the festive table something which is either eaten on the spot or stored away in the bag that swings at the end of a stick over each boy's shoulder.

The *Dyngus* songs are all very much alike, containing good wishes, requests for gifts and food, or threats in case the requests should be denied. A popular *Dyngus* song is the following:

> *Your duck has told me*
> *That you've baked a cake*
> *Your hen has told me that*
> *She's laid you a basket and a half of eggs*
> *Your sow has told me that you've killed her son*
> *If not her son then her little daughter*
> *Give me something if only a bit of her fat*
> *Who will not be generous today*
> *Let him not count on heaven.*

Or the boys, dressed as gypsies and soldiers, may come to the doors singing:

Let us into the house
For we are here on the Smigus
And give us what you have in mind to give us.

On leaving they cry out, '*Smigus* Splash goes the water!' At this signal everyone seizes whatever vessel he has and pours water on the host, his wife, or anyone else within reach.

Another amusement of Easter Monday is going about with 'the Bear'. The Bear is one of the young men in the village disguised in a 'bearskin' made of pea vines. He wears a bell on his head and is accompanied by another young man carrying a basket for the offerings they receive in their pilgrimage from door to door, asking 'gifts for the Bear'. At the end of the tour the Bear is 'drowned'—that is, the masquerader is drenched, or ducked in a nearby stream or pond where his coat of pea vines will remain. This drowning ceremony is probably a variant of drowning the straw image Marzanna, representing winter.

The girls make rounds of their own on Easter Monday. On that day they go from cottage to cottage carrying a freshly cut evergreen tree or branch, known as *gaj* or *gaik*. They too sing traditional songs in return for food or other small gifts. The songs make clear the belief that the new year starts with spring, and that the *gaj*, bedecked with ribbons and flowers, holds its essence and its promise.

In the green little tree
Dappled with gold
Is summer and May—
God give us good fortune.

Mistress, the new Summer is in the hall
If you'd like to see it
You must give it something.

And again:

> *Our green little tree, beautifully decked*
> *Goes everywhere*
> *For it is proper that it should*
> *We go with it to the manor house*
> *Wishing good fortune, good health*
> *For this new year*
> *Which God has given us.*

The bringing in of the *gaj* may take place at other times, from Lent through Easter or even through Whitsuntide. Formerly in Silesia or Little Poland it was brought back to the village by the girls as they returned from drowning Marzanna. In approaching the village they would sing:

> *We have taken little Marzanka out of the village—*
> *We are bringing a* gaj *into the village,*

Usually, however, the two ceremonies are separate.

Dyngus, this 'second day' of Easter, is a time of great sociability, especially if warm and sunny weather invites the villagers to saunter and visit each other. The younger married couples call on the older ones, bringing gifts of coloured eggs and fine wheaten rolls. On entering the cottage, they offer greetings of the season, are welcomed with warmth and ceremony, and offered delicacies from the Easter table. Their visit will be returned on the evening of the same day or the one following. The conviviality, like the abundance of food, is an exception to the peasant rule and part of the contrast between holidays and plain days.

Easter week is known as *przewodni tydzien* or *przewodnia niedziela,* transition or transference week, and ends with Quasimodogenitit Sunday. Throughout Poland any hard work is prohibited during this week, particularly on Thursday since that is the day devoted exclusively to the memory of the dead. Ill luck befalls those who disobey the rule. One story is told of a farmer who ploughed on that Thursday and was swallowed up by the earth, together with his plough, oxen, and driver. If one puts his ear to the ground he will hear the unfortunate driver and farmer calling for help. In some places, people especially avoid working with linen or yarn on that day, 'in order not to get dust in the eyes of the souls'.

Part of the welcome to spring, though not strictly part of the Easter cycle, is St. George's Day on April 21. St. George is one of the best loved saints, hero of spring and of the sun. He is often pictured as a beautiful youth in armour, mounted on a white charger, fearless defender of the Christian faith.

People of the Krakow region think of him as a hussar. They say that during his life on earth he was a soldier. At the command of the Holy Virgin he saved an innocent maiden from a dragon and as a reward received the moon for his abode. Ever since then, they say, 'St. George lives on the moon and plays the lute to the glory of God'.

In workaday customs and thought, St. George is seen as a more intimate figure, and a highly important one. He is guardian of spring vegetation and of the flocks and herds. With his keys he opens the earth to release the grasses, grains and flowers that have been imprisoned during the winter. The farmer says too, 'St. George will open wide the frogs' mouths', meaning that after his day the spring chorus of frogs will sound again.

St. George is also a bringer of rain and dew. Young people and farm animals must bathe in the dew of his day, which will make them strong and healthy.

In some sections of Poland, 'St. George's' is a complete holiday and no work is done at all. Fires are often lit in the yards the night before, to keep witches away from the animals. They burn all night and the farmhands sit around them, playing their fifes and singing. Branches of birch are put in front of the cottages and thorn branches are placed

E

before the stables, or crosses are marked on stable doors with tar—all in order to keep out witches.

A feature of St. George's Day met with in some form in all Slavonic lands is the excursion into the fields. These excursions may take the form of processions accompanied by ceremony and prayer, with all the villagers except the very old and the very young taking part. Twigs of the willow blessed on Palm Sunday are stuck into the ground to protect the grain from hail and from 'unclean powers'; bones saved from the Easter meats are buried in the soil to prevent the spread of weeds; and shells from the coloured Easter eggs are buried to promote growth. After this ceremony, a cloth is spread in the field, and blessed food remaining from Easter is eaten, with accompanying draughts of vodka.

In some places, the farmers accompanied by their households march around the fields and roll on the ground before eating. Elsewhere, a special *pierog*, baked for the occasion, is the principal food of the feast and is used to foretell the harvests. Made of dough and filled with meat, cheese, cabbage, or some other filling, the *pierog* is a favourite food aside from its ceremonial features, and one that has become popular in the restaurants of New York as well as of Warsaw.

At times, especially in recent years, the excursion to the fields may be a mere party given over to singing, merry-making, dancing, and rolling on the ground. All this is great fun but the important thing is that it will help to bring a good harvest—especially the rolling on the ground.

St. George's is the traditional day for the sowing of flax. There is a proverb, 'If you would have good linen, sow your flax on St. George's'.

As special guardian of spring vegetation, St. George gives particular care to the winter corn, which should be at least high enough on his day for a crow to hide in. Peasants who have fields of winter corn go to them on that day to see how it is progressing—'to hear what the corn is saying'. St. George maintains his guardianship until 'the heads form' on the corn. Then he commits it to St. Peter and returns to his regular duties as protector of flocks and herds. He is thought of literally as a shepherd, moving unseen about the fields, 'pasturing the cows, protecting them with his keen-nosed dog and his sharp stick from the marauding beasts and the witch-hag.'

In many places, the animals are driven to pasture for the first time on his day, with due ceremony. They are decked with greenery, shining trinkets and red flowers or ribbons— for the colour red is thought to ward off evil spells. The cows and also the cowherds are doused with water, so that the cows will give abundant milk. To protect the cows from sickness and mishaps, they are lashed with the 'Easter switch', and also made to bathe in St. George's dew.

The first of May, a springtime festival in its own right, is also the feast of St. Philip and St. Jacob the Apostle, patrons of marriageable girls. It combines the elements of welcome to springtime, mating rites and games, and tricks reminiscent of April Fool's Day in some other countries.

On the eve of May Day the village youths go out during the evening and play practical jokes, often involving scarecrows or images called *filipki*—'little Philips'. Pulling up gate posts, stopping up bee hives, throwing wagon-poles down chimney-flues are common May Day pranks. In certain regions a 'little Philip' may be thrown through the roof to frighten the girls; or the boys may tease the girls by placing scarecrows before their cottages as a grim warning of late marriage.

The more amiable custom of placing a *majek* or 'little May' before the cottage of a popular girl is found throughout southwestern Poland. The *majek* is a tall smooth pole, a true maypole as it is known in Anglo-Saxon tradition. A small juniper bush or evergreen is tied to the top of the pole, which is then tasselled with ribbons and flowers.

The young men parade down the village streets, singing martial songs to the accompaniment of music and consulting loudly between songs about who should be crowned. They finally place the decorated pole before the cottage of the girl chosen, whereupon her delighted mother rushes out and invites the party of young men into the house. Soon other girls of the village come hurrying to the scene, and all join in dancing.

The May Day ceremony has numerous variations in different regions. In one part of southeastern Poland the young men during the night, place before the home of the girl they wish to honour, two 'mays'—fir trees from which the lower branches have been pruned. In the morning the young men stand in front of the house singing a song that begins: 'With what intention, in memory of what, place they the mays?' They also sing a song to St. Philip and St. Jacob: 'We place the mays, asking for your love'. At the head of their procession walks the *Starosta*, the leader in the district, bearing on a plate a floral wreath decorated with ribbons. Among the followers a group of girls, carrying another 'may', break from the throng and dance about it.

In another variation, the young men of the Poznan district select two tall smooth poles and, before decorating them in the usual way, tie the kerchiefs of their favourite girls at the top. When the ceremonies begin, the men climb the poles, take down the kerchiefs, and collect forfeits from the girls to whom they belong. At Whitsuntide the mays are 'undressed', after which the young men are entertained by the parents of the girls they have honoured.

Although auspicious for love, the first of May is considered generally unlucky for husbandry, and care is taken not to do certain things on that day. Potatoes, for example, should not be planted on May 1st. Oats and flax on the contrary do well, and parsley will flourish if sown on May Day, even though frost should follow. Hens are not set to eggs on that day, for the eggs would be likely to hatch '*filipki*'—deformed, abnormal fledglings. In some places, throughout the whole year, hens are not set to eggs on the day of the week on which St. Philip's falls.

Like many other saints' days, the feast of St. Philip and St. Jacob is the subject of rhymed sayings and proverbs dealing chiefly with the weather, and pointing out the farmers' principal tasks. For example, literally translated:

> *Rain on the first of May*
> *Is a prophecy of bad weather.*

> *Rain on the first of May—*
> *Misery in harvest.*

> *If the first of May burns*
> *The mares will be lean.*

> *Frost on the first of May*
> *Promises a bounteous crop.*

> *Clouds on St. Jacob's—*
> *Wagonloads of snow.*

The Virgin Mary, important all the year round, is honoured especially in the spring. As in all Catholic countries, the whole month of May is dedicated to her, with special ceremonies such as adorning her altars and shrines, both indoors and outdoors. On May 3 the Poles celebrate the Feast of the Virgin Mary, Queen of the Polish Crown—an appellation which figures also in the Polish version of the litany.

The popular names for the Annunciation, on March 25, reflect not only the peasant's unending concern with the weather, but also his belief that the Holy Mother is one of those who watch over the proper course of the seasons. One name for this day is Our Lady of the Brooks because from then on the ice begins to break in the streams, loosing the spring freshets. The Holy Mother, like some of the lesser saints, helps to warm the air, open the earth, bring back life to the wakening vegetation. The giving of life and support to nature and to man is especially appropriate to her character and her importance, discussed more fully in connection with the late summer and early fall.

Like all important holidays, the feasts of Our Lady are watched for signs of weather and omens pertaining to the crops.

SUMMER

Here is the new summer
Here is the month of May
Give luck, oh Lord!

SUMMER BRINGS A blast of heat and a sustained battle against weeds, elements, the armies of vermin that stalk the fields. Hail-storms, droughts, floods, may threaten the crops. Against such perils the farmer seeks help from heaven and the saints, as well as from whatever magical practice or pagan ritual is within his grasp—and needless to say, from his own efforts.

The period just before the first crops are gathered is called *przednowek*, 'before new'. This is the time when hunger can become most fierce. Supplies dwindle and sometimes give out before the first of the early crops are ready. So strong is the dread of 'before new', that even prosperous peasants who have not actually suffered from it feel its shadow, and speak of it as if for them too its hardships were real.

Yet summer is a good time. Second only to spring as a season of hard work, it is second only to spring in the affections of the peasant. It is good work they do in summer, and the sun is bright and harvest is ahead.

The Green Holidays, *Zielone Swiatki*, mark the swing of the year into summer. As the name suggests, they celebrate the victorious season and its green glory. Like all the Polish peasant's seasonal holidays, they are designed to bring about successful farming through the help of the supernatural, heavenly or otherwise.

In honour of the Green Holidays, churches, houses, cottages, farm buildings and yards are decorated with branches of birch, ash or fir. Sometimes small trees are placed next to altars, doors, windows, and gates. The floors and enclosed yards are strewn with green calamus, sweet flag, pine needles and flowers. Sprays of calamus are put on window sills. Planetree branches are taken out into the fields to safeguard the grain against destruction by hail.

On the Green Holidays, as on May Day, the 'placing of mays' is practised. A young man takes a birch sapling to the home of a girl and plants it in front of her house as a token of affection and a sign of serious matrimonial intentions. Girls who have a bad reputation receive dry branches or a cluster of noxious weeds.

This is above all, however, the holiday of herdsmen and farmers. In many places the cowherd who is the first to get his cattle to pasture on the first day of the Green Holidays becomes the king of the shepherds, and a girl is chosen for his queen. If two men should arrive at the pasture at the same time, a foot race is staged to pick the winner.

The king and queen of the festivities receive offerings of flowers, ribbons and peacock plumes from which a wreath is made for each of them. Bouquets are made from these same leaves and flowers for the 'officials' in the royal retinue. The king appoints a marshal, a royal cook and a cup-bearer; and a fife is sounded to invite everyone to a feast by the fire.

In the evening the finest ox in the village is garlanded with flowers and green-stuff, and led through the village streets to the sound of music and singing. The marshal heads the procession, wearing around his waist as badge of office a ceremonial towel, long and richly embroidered. Behind him come the young girls, strewing field flowers along the way.

The entire village greets the royal procession as it goes from house to house, and finally leads the way to the tavern or to one of the larger cottages for a final round of singing, dancing and drinking.

Meanwhile the unfortunate shepherd who was the last to reach the pasture has been crowned with a humiliating wreath of straw. He is doomed to watch all the cattle for three days while the others make merry.

This is another of the holidays on which a ceremonial march through the fields is staged. The Green Holiday pilgrimage through the fields is one of the most important, but there are processions also on Corpus Christi and St. Mark's, as well as on St. George's. In fact the Poles have a leaning toward processions which are apt to figure in almost any celebration. Figures dressed in green are carried in the procession for *Zielone Swiatki,* and the marchers chant a plea for good crops. The green figure is called the 'May princess' and her passage through the fields will help to make a good harvest.

A live princess may also be chosen. In the Podlasie region, for example, the most beautiful girl in the village is made princess, and six or eight older girls are selected as her attendants. A crown of rue, periwinkle and other wild flowers is placed on her head and she is led with her retinue along the boundaries of the fields. They sing:

> *Where the princess walks*
> *There the wheat will grow*
> *Where the princess walks not*
> *There wheat will not grow.*

At the end of the tour the procession stops before the manor house or before the house of one of the wealthier peasants and sing, among others, this song:

The princess went a-Maying—
Whose rye stood so high?
Our master's rye stood so high.
Pay the princess her fee
And let her cut the rye.

In the mountain regions, the farmer takes a pitcher of holy water and an aspergillum, goes into the fields and sprinkles the budding grain, asking God to protect his yield from rain, wind and frost.

Formerly great piles of dead trees were burned in the fields as a part of the *Zielone Swiatki* ceremony. Though this custom has ceased, the belief that fire has power to shield cattle from harm through pestilence, sickness or bad magic is still popular throughout Poland. It has been noted in connection with St. George's Day and appears in many other rites.

The dew of special days is also a safety charm. During *Zielone Swiatki* women wishing their cows to yield abundant milk, fumigate the milking pail with herbs made magic by boiling all night long. Then, just before daybreak, they run out with the milk pail on their heads, to a crossroad where they gather enough dew to mix with the herb brew. As they gather the dew they say three times: 'I wish not what is another's, but I will not give up my own'.

Returning to their cottages before sunrise, they mix the herb infusion with the gathered dew, sprinkle the liquid mixture with flour and then offer it to the cows with this incantation: 'and there shall be milk and the witch shall not take it away'.

On the second of the Green Holidays in certain regions of Poland an ox is driven through the village, with a straw effigy placed on its back. This effigy is dressed in cap, boots and a coat. A crowd of boys running behind cry '*Rodus, Rodus.*'

At one time, no doubt, the figure represented a person who had died. Rodus is a diminutive variation of Rod, a divinity of the Eastern Slavs and one who represented a venerated ancestor. Other touches throughout the spring and early

summer holidays suggest practices relating to ancestor worship in early pagan days; but with the passage of time such
survivals have lost their memorial character, at least so far
as the peasants are concerned.

Another second day observance found in various places
contrasts curiously with the crowning of the first shepherd on
the first day. Boys of the village seize the shepherd who was
first to let his cattle into the fields after winter, smear his face
with tar, cover him with a cloth and tie him to a wheel-
barrow. They then lead him from farm to farm, accompanied by musicians. They strike him lightly with green
boughs and crack a whip over his head as they go, crying
over and over, '*wieziema smolarza, a do gospodarza*'. 'we are
carrying the tarman to the farmer'. At each farm they receive
offerings of bread, cheese, eggs and pork fat. Finally they take
the tarman to a river or a pond and throw him in to
wash himself. Then follows a gay party at the village
tavern.

The pattern is similar to that of many processions and
punitive duckings, including the ducking of the Bear at
Shrovetide. In this case, however, the man who won a
coveted 'first' is punished—in line with the frequent feeling
among Polish peasants that no one should stand out above
his fellows, and that if he does he should get his 'come-
uppance'. The ducking ceremony is commonly associated
with fertility, agricultural and human.

Summer is not a season of many big festivals. The days of
the saints are duly observed, and care is taken to plant the
right crops on auspicious days and to avoid doing important
work on days of ill omen.

Having taken over the fields of grain from St. George, St.
Peter—whose day falls in June—watches over their progress.
He must be encouraged to struggle against the obstacles

placed in his way by the prophet Elisha, who rules over the elements. St. Gregory works diligently in the kitchen gardens, with special care for the cabbage plants. Benedict has the peas in his keeping, Mark the flax, Philip the buckwheat. This is of course another way of saying that those crops should be planted on the day of the saint responsible for them, and that the saints must be kept mindful of their duties through the summer, by prayers and appropriate remembrances.

There is a special practice for St. Jacob's Day, on July 25— a different St. Jacob from the one whose day falls on May 1. Farmers whose hens lay more than a *mendel*—that is, fifteen— eggs on St. Jacob's, give half of them to the poor, who go about with baskets crying ,'In honour of St. Jacob, put some eggs in the basket—for this the saint will give you cash aplenty.'

St. John's Day, on June 24, marks the peak of the summer. The special promise of St. John is youth, love, and general fertility. Because of his concern with fertility, he—in common with several others—has power as a bringer of rain.

According to old Slavonic legends, the Eve of St. John's is fraught with miracles and magic. Animals talk to each other with human voices. The earth becomes transparent and shows the enchanted riches in its depths, glowing with celestial fires. In wild ravines, the barren fern blooms at midnight with a flaming flower. Fortune and happiness will come to anyone who finds it, but the flower is so hidden that it can be discovered only through great good luck. Moreover, it is guarded by demonic figures, who, with hisses and screeches, prevent one from plucking it.

Strange things happen to the sun on St. John's Eve. It 'bathes' in the river, 'dances' and 'plays' in the sky. In Upper Silesia, offerings of cake are made to the sun. Girls dance 'after the sun'—that is, following the direction of its course, and as they dance, they sing: 'Play, sun, play, here are your little suns!'

On St. John's Eve, phenomena natural and supernatural acquire special significance. Certain plants take on magical properties. Camomile, white clover, and mugwort gathered before sunset are an unmatched remedy for rheumatism and other illnesses. Certain flowers and grasses, made into wreaths, will forecast one's fate in marriage.

The fire of this night is not ordinary fire. It must be 'live' or 'new'—that is, freshly struck by rubbing sticks or flint. Objects snatched from a St. John's Eve fire are believed to have the power of warding off lightning or sickness and bringing about successful marriages.

Devils and witches also command unusual power on this night. They gather on 'Bald Mountains' for feasts and revelry. They play tricks, do mischief to human beings and cattle, take milk away from cows, bring drought and other disasters. Therefore people take steps to counteract their evil influences. The shepherds bring their cattle and sheep in earlier than usual. They fasten to their horns a wreath made of clover and the flowers called 'blue bottles'. Even geese wear tiny wreaths skilfully woven of darnel and daisies.

Bunches of mugwort and wormwood are hung under the roof of barns and stables, to keep the witch from coming at night and milking the cows—for men have seen witches dancing on broomsticks and cavorting at crossroads, in anticipation of the night's revelry.

People along the Polish seashore sprinkle their boats with holy water and strew the bottoms of their boats with branches of the plane-tree on St. John's Eve. They weave into their nets herbs and grasses that were blessed on Corpus Christi, earlier in June. All this is done to render impotent the evil powers that only wait to raise the wind, rouse the sea, tangle the dragnets or even drown the fisherman.

festivity but are designed primarily to add to the farm's prosperity.

In some regions of Poland the head of the family takes a spoonful of peas when they are brought in, puts them on the windowsill, knocks on the pane, and calls out: 'Wolf, Wolf, come to the peas, if you come not to the peas, come not until the new year!' and, while eating the peas the feasters will pull at each other's hair, exclaiming, 'Twine, peas, twine!' While eating the cabbage, they strike each other over the head with their spoons, saying, 'Fold, cabbage, fold!'—that is, make good, firm heads. Eating the millet seed they shout, '*Kic sie, proso, kic!*'—'Make tufts, millet, grow full!' Through all the eating, a spoonful of food is set aside for the barn and household animals.

More elaborate mealtime incantations are found in some parts of Poland, as among other Slavonic peoples. One is pronounced while the farmer leads the grown members of the household in a procession three times around the table, wafting incense. The children recite the following verse from under the table:

> *Cackle, cackle, a hundred hens!*
> *Honk, honk, a hundred geese!*
> *Quack, quack, a hundred ducks!*
> *Moo, moo, a hundred oxen!*

This magic onomatopeia is carried through all the list of barnyard beasts and fowls, to the pleasure of the children and the presumable profit of the farm.

Another observance consists of dialogue between husband and wife. Crossing himself three times, the farmer sits in the place of honour—the place where the altar stands or where the holiest picture hangs. His wife, facing him across the feast-laden table, questions him and he answers.

'Do you see me?'
'I do not.'

'May you not see the light
For the stacks, the bushels, the wagons!'

Then the husband questions the wife:

'Do you see me?'
'I do not.'
'May you not see the light for the watermelons, the cabbages, the beets!'

The serving of the *kutja,* at the end of the meal, is always attended by ceremony. The housewife brings it to the table, steaming in a large bowl. Her husband, standing, makes the sign of the cross over it and offers a prayer. The wife follows this with a short prayer in which she asks the health of all and begs God to give them good crops in the coming year.

If the head of the household takes a spoonful of the *kutja* and throws it at the ceiling, the number of wheat grains that adhere will indicate the number of bushels of grain that will be harvested in the year to come. In some places the wife goes to the window with a spoonful of *kutja* and 'bids' the frost. Knocking on the pane she calls out, 'Freeze not my seedlings, my cucumbers, my squash and pumpkins, my carrots, my beets, nor any of that which God will permit us to sow and to plant'.

Next to thought for the crops, length of life and marriage are chief concerns. The Christmas Eve supper, like many important occasions, serves as a time for divining one's personal fate. All pull straws from under the tablecloth. A long straw foretells a long life, a short one means a short life. If a girl pulls a straw with a tuft, she will find a husband during the year. (Not content with this hint, she is likely also to count fence pickets and pour melted wax into water during the holiday, to learn more about him.)

When the meal is over, all continue to sit at the table until a signal is given for them to leave in a body. The first to rise from the Christmas feast is expected to die before the next Christmas Eve. Therefore—as so often among the Poles—it is advisable that nobody be first.

Practice varies regarding the remains of the feast, but care is taken to treat them with respect and to make full use of their beneficent properties. An almost universal custom dictates that some of the food be reserved, either at the beginning or the end of the meal, for the departed ancestors, as part of their entertainment during this period when they revisit the familiar haunts of their lifetime. The Christmas observances, like so many in Poland, reveal the assumption that a feast is not entirely over when the eating is done, and people are not permanently gone when they have been buried.

Crumbs from the festive table are saved to be sown in the garden at springtime. The grass that grows on the spot where they were thrown is believed to have medicinal value.

In many places the family visit the farm animals after supper, taking them Christmas wafers and scraps of the food remaining from the feast, 'so that they too may feel the holiday spirit'. At every turn the Polish peasant shows his regard for his animals, as helpers, as friends, almost as human beings. Perhaps the barnyard members of the family appreciate more the other offerings brought to them on this occasion—the hay that was under the table-cloth and some of the straw that was strewn on the cottage floor. These are fed to them partly out of thrift, but chiefly in the belief that they have become imbued with the tonic power possessed by everything connected with Christmas.

From the animals, in regions where this is customary, the family proceed to the orchard to perform rites inducing fertility in the trees. Straw from the festal floor is wrapped around them so that they will bear lavishly. The wrapping— which in some places is done at a different point during the Christmas holidays—is performed with ceremony. The farmer himself may wrap the trees, or it may be his wife, the farmhands, or other young men or women, depending on the local tradition.

Striking or threatening the trees is equally general, as in many other countries. It may take the form of knocking on the tree with the bare fists or with a stick. In one region a farmhand wraps each barren tree with straw, after which the master knocks several times on it with these words: 'May you be so fertile that you will have more fruit than leaves'. In another region, the young farmhands and girls put ropes of straw about the trees that have been barren and strike them several times with a walking stick, saying, 'Thou shalt bear and I will walk in thee'. In still another region, the peasants vary the more usual procedure by shaking, caressing and kissing the barren trees, coaxing them to bear.

Elsewhere, a threatening gesture may be made with an axe. The farmer lifts the axe, making as if to strike the tree, and asking sternly, 'Wilt thou bear or wilt thou not?' Other members of the household answer for the tree, promising that it will bear, whereupon the farmer will lower his axe giving the tree a year in which to mend its ways. Needless to say the tree is never cut. The impulse to conserve is reinforced by the generally held belief that one who cuts down a fruit tree will either die soon himself or lose a member of his family.

These customs of shaking, striking and wrapping trees with straw from the festive table, are probably vestiges of primitive spring rites to induce fertility. In many places such ceremonies are performed later, at various times up to Easter. The custom of lashing people, particularly the young, is thought to derive from the same primitive observance.

After the welfare of stables and orchards has been attended to, the evening is given to stories and songs. Relatives and neighbours may come to visit, and waits may arrive to sing their carols and receive sweets from the tree and the table. At midnight the churchbells ring out, summoning all but

the youngest children to the *Pasterka*, or Shepherds Mass—the Midnight Mass which closes the holy Eve and ushers in the day of Christ's birth.

Christmas day is generally marked by less formal ceremony than its Eve. For many of the important festivals the day proper is the aftermath of the Eve, rather than the Eve being merely the fore-runner of the day.

Visits to friends and relatives are made on Christmas day, and waits may make the rounds of the cottages. Although some carol-singing is done on Christmas Day and Christmas Eve, it is nevertheless more likely to begin the day after Christmas. The exchange of gifts, so important in Great Britain and the United States, is not a part of the Polish Christmas celebration.

A great feature of Christmas day and of the Christmas season is the *szopka*—a miniature puppet theatre made of cardboard and elaborately decorated with ribbons. It takes the form of a church and includes one or more stages set with scenes of biblical origin. It includes also, however, some very secular performances and a great deal of horseplay which delights both the children and their elders.

If the *szopka* is very small, it is carried on a stick by one of the boys in the procession that accompanies it from house to house. Larger ones are built on a platform and carried by two or four boys, or else trundled on a cart.

The *szopka* is typically an out-of-door performance, but if the weather is very cold, the players and their companions may be invited into the house to get warm and perhaps to enjoy some refreshment. The 'actors' on the miniature stages are puppets ingeniously whittled out of wood and dressed in characteristic costumes. They have flexible hands and legs, which are moved by means of sticks inserted in the stage floors. A puppeteer moves them, making them speak with his own voice, and the performance is accompanied by music supplied by the boys in the procession.

The many figures represented on the stage of the *szopka* vary according to locality. In the Krakow region, from which the best known come, the first figure to appear on the stage is a Polish nobleman, bearing a rusty *karabela,* or ancient pike. A dignified and elaborately dressed matron comes forth to meet him, they make a joint bow and then go into a spirited *polonaise.* They are followed by a Cossack who amuses the spectators by dancing on his haunches in typical Cossack style, flinging his legs out after the fashion of the *trepak.* He is joined by his lady and they end their performance with a lively hop. Next appear a German in tight breeches, a mountaineer with a bear, and a wandering workman. Finally Herod—the most popular figure of the *szopka*—enters with his mace. Death comes and puts his scythe around Herod's neck, then the Devil arrives demanding Death for his own. A lively brawl develops, during which Herod either commits suicide or manages to save himself. If he is saved, he will turn to the audience and end the performance with a request for donations. If not, the request will be made by the boys, perhaps in one of the innumerable asking songs that characterize the lively and tuneful processional of many Polish holidays.

The Nativity scene is frequently portrayed in the *szopka,* often in the form of tableaux. But the gayer and more rowdy dramas are the most popular, and in recent years have inspired Polish artists and illustrators. There was hardly a city child in pre-war Poland who did not cherish a picture book full of vivid, picturesque scenes representing the Christmas-time spectacles.

The city children themselves have Christmas dramas, called *jaselka.* They are morality plays depicting the scenes of the Nativity, and acted by children.

Christmas carol-singing, which continues through Epiphany, may begin on Christmas Eve or, in some places, on

Christmas day. More often, however, the carols begin the day after Christmas on St. Stephen's Day—known in Poland as *drugie swieto,* the second holiday. The custom of *chodzenie po kolendzie,* going about carol-singing, is practised everywhere in Poland. The carols sung are beautiful, numerous, characteristically Polish, and performed with a verve borne of high spirits and thorough training.

Well in advance of Christmas, the carollers gather and choose as 'teacher' a young man thoroughly versed in both the holy and lay carol. They meet frequently and go through a rigid schooling, rehearsing many songs arranged in four part harmony. They also go through a number of dance routines, for dancing is part and parcel of good carol-singing. Both dancing and music seem to be an integral part of the Polish peasant, and he feels them as inseparably bound together.

The carols fall into two groups, the religious and the secular. The religious ones have as their theme the Nativity, announcing the birth of Christ or celebrating incidents drawn from its story. They are most apt to be sung before the cottages where there are no girls. Secular carols are most often sung for households where young girls are present. They are laudatory, telling of the deeds of some hero, praising the farmer's wife, his riches, his generosity, or perhaps the beauty of a girl. A principal theme in secular carols is success in husbandry, for which the help of God and the saints is often invoked.

The secular carol ends with a rousing wish for the good fortune of the person to whom it is directed, and many carry more than a hint that some offering would be appreciated.

> *For happiness, for health, for this New Year*
> *That wheat, that peas might bear*
> *And rye, and all, and millet*
> *That you might not walk barefoot—*
> *Cakes have been baked here, and bread, we were told*
> *Gracious, beautiful lady, give some to us!*

Variants of this begin with the request: 'The boys were saying that you have baked cakes. . . .'

There are also carols for particular persons, under special circumstances: carols for a widower, a widow, for a youth away from home, for the dead. All of these are in the form of songs of praise, ending with the usual good wishes, and serving something of the function of greeting cards in Great Britain and the United States. They may be the regularly sung carols, with a few special lines of phrases inserted.

Where the custom of carol-singing still retains its ancient and solemn character, it is considered more than an ordinary ceremony, and is surrounded by an elaborate system of regulations. In some places the singers may be youths or married men, and the chief requirement is ability to sing and to master the art of carol-singing. Elsewhere the requirements are more rigid, and to be one of the waits takes on the aura of membership in a fraternity.

During the last few decades, however, the solemnity that marked the carol-singing of former times has slowly given way to a spirit of fun, expressed in mischievous pranks if the waits are not properly rewarded. In many regions now the waits are mere boys and not young men as before. The boys sing only church carols and carry with them from house to house the traditional paper star hung from a long stick. It is made of coloured cardboard, so constructed that it revolves like a pinwheel. Often one or two of the boys will be masked as a goat, bear or pony, to add to the entertainment.

The same sort of procession accompanies the *szopka,* and since the spirit of the carols has become more frivolous, the waits themselves may carry a *szopka* with them.

Throughout Poland on St. Stephen's the peasants throw grain at one another to bring a good harvest. Members of the family throw grain at each other, at friends, and at the animals in the stable, In church the congregation may

Young people throughout Poland spend St. John's Eve in playing games and kindling the magical fires. If they are close to a river or pond, young girls cast on the water wreaths to which are fixed lighted candles, so that their course may be followed. The girls watch from shore while boys, darting over the water in small, swift boats, retrieve the wreaths with the help of long sticks. From the course and fate of the wreaths, auguries of marriage are made.

At times the young people also throw themselves into the water. Young men and girls leap by pairs over the fires, then all run from fire to water. After a dip they dress and return to sing and dance and feast around the fire. On this evening the correct costume for the girls is a long, loose white robe, and their flowing garments present a haunting, unearthly picture against the blackness of the night.

The songs of St. John's Eve have a strangely drawn out and wistful melody. Their text is closely allied to that of wedding songs, as befits the songs of a saint who specializes in love and fertility. One of the most melodious and most frequently sung says:

> The leaves are falling all around, all around
> Time for you, young farmer
> To seek you a wife, seek you a wife.

Although autumn is the real harvest time, the very early crops are gathered in the summer—some as early as St. John's. St. Lawrence's Day, on August 10, however, is more strongly associated with harvest. 'On St. Lawrence's one must go to the rye field with one's scythe', was an old saying; and today one still may hear, 'St. Lawrence makes one go out to the rye.'

In late summer and early fall, several days are dedicated to the Virgin Mary. On Assumption Day, August 15, in addition to the ceremonies of the day itself, the harvest wreath is often taken to the church to be blessed, for use later

in the harvest festival. Later, on September 8, is the Nativity of the Virgin.

The Holy Mother occupies a place second only to that of her divine Son, in the peasant's hierarchy. Her role is that of mother to man as well as to God, and the intensity of her worship is closely linked to the deep respect for human motherhood. Because of her tenderness, Mary is appealed to on behalf of the weak, the sick, the innocent, and those of high purpose, such as soldiers setting forth to battle.

She has more holidays in the course of the year than any of the saints. No less than five of them are observed in Poland with extensive and solemn ceremony. In addition to the three named above, there are the Purification on February 2 and the Annunciation on March 25.

Moreover, May is her special month, as mentioned earlier, and Saturday her special day throughout the year. Tasks in which her help is particularly sought should be undertaken on Saturday. In olden times lights were burned before her picture on that day.

In Poland, as elsewhere, more churches are named for the Virgin Mary than for any other heavenly figure. Miraculous pictures of her are venerated throughout the country—one count sets the number as high as one thousand and fifty. The pictures at Czestochowa and Wilno are known throughout the entire Catholic world. Following the custom initiated by Gregory III some of these pictures have been crowned, the first being the famous Black Madonna of Czestochowa, which was crowned with great pomp and ceremony on September 8, 1717.

This smoke-darkened Byzantine painting, according to legend, miraculously survived fire during the siege of Czestochowa, and became famous for working miracles. For centuries it has been an object of pious pilgrimage, in fact the

most popular of them all. Each year, in the autumn, pilgrims set forth to pray before the Black Madonna. Some go for expiation, some in gratitude for blessings received, some in hope of blessings to come—and some, especially the devout aged beggars, go out of sheer holiness. They come from all parts of Poland, setting out from their homes as soon as the harvest is in. It is the tradition of this pilgrimage that it must be made on foot and, despite the rugged individualism of the Pole, it is made in groups, each with its own cross-bearer. They chant prayers and pious songs as they go, or walk to the accompaniment of band music. They help each other along the road, sharing meals together, and generally displaying a spirit of exalted camaraderie quite different from the approved behaviour for ordinary situations. Such pilgrimages are voluntary, in contrast to the more perfunctory confessional. They may entail sacrifice and even hardship. And they are among the most genuine expressions of the Polish peasant's religious feeling.

The Virgin figures in countless popular legends, always as the benefactor of the weak, the oppressed, the burdened and the lost. Often she is called 'the Protectress'. She is viewed as a special helper of the farmer. One legend tells that when the Virgin was fleeing into Egypt, escaping the soldiers of Herod, she came upon a peasant sowing his wheat. Taking the seed-bag from the astonished farmer she sowed all of his fields with her own hands, telling him that he would cut his wheat the next morning.

The following day, as the farmer began to harvest his miraculous crop, the soldiers of Herod approached, asking about the woman and child who were said to have gone that way. The farmer replied that he had indeed seen a woman and child go by, but that had been while he was sowing his wheat. Discouraged, the soldiers gave up their pursuit of the Mother and Child.

Women also feel that Mary is their especial friend. When their husbands beat them, they pray to her rather than to a male divinity because, as the proverb has it, 'A man will always stand up for a man'.

Mary not only protects humankind from each other and from the elements, she also intercedes in heaven for the weak and wretched. If a saint is remiss in his duty, the peasant may pray to the Holy Mother for help. She will even plead for them with God, as a mother intercedes for her children when the father is stern in his justice.

One characteristic tale about Mary shows her protecting, not men, but neglected flowers. It explains the 'ice flowers' that form on frosty window-panes on very cold days. People believe that these are the ones that did not have a chance to bloom during the summer, and that they were first created for trees such as pines, spruce, hemlock and firs.

When the Lord created the world, it is told, the last thing he did was to send the flowers to earth. He had so many that he couldn't send them all. There were fruit trees and all other flowering plants, but the needle-bearing trees were left without blossoms.

In order to console them He told them that summer is not the only season on earth. There would be a winter, too, when snow-white clouds would cover the fields and all the other trees would be naked and bare. Only they would remain fresh and green, for the beauty of the forest and the happiness of man.

So the Lord took care of the trees, but there were still the little flowers left, the ones that should have bloomed on those trees. Then Mary said, 'Oh Lord, let those flowers go to the dwellings of men and stay with them the whole winter.'

The Lord was very pleased. Since then, those flowers adorn the window-panes of houses, like millions of tiny stars.

Nothing can happen to those flowers for the whole winter long. When the warm air during the day erases them, they hover in the air and come back at night. This was the Lord's will, through the intervention of Mary Mother.

Autumn

From the green forest grove
The harvesters come
They carry the golden wreath
The work of the harvest maids.

We have cut everything
From boundary to boundary
Look, master, look
There is not a thing in the field.

THE REAL END of the year is harvest time, a period of rejoicing overshadowed by the onset of winter. It is good to gather in the crops, to sell them, and for the moment to be relieved of hunger if not of want.

But the long cold winter is drawing near—a no-man's-land of the calendar, between the end of one crop year and the beginning of the next.

It is appropriate that the autumn, which begins with gathering in the life-giving grain, should end with the Feast of the Dead. For it is the season that bridges the gap between the fertility of summer and the frozen sterility of the year's death.

In the lives of an agricultural people the beginning of the harvest is bound to be a major event and a happy one. A large number of practices are carried out to insure the best possible results. Shrewdly the peasant leaves nothing undone —neither Christian prayer nor pre-Christian ritual. In his own belief, there is no clearcut distinction between the two. Witches and evil spirits take their place in a hierarchy that includes also the Devil.

F

It is only since World War I that the harvest customs have weakened perceptibly, but until World War II they continued to flourish in villages removed from urban influence, and in some of the larger estates where many hands worked without benefit of modern machinery. They have been weakened less by falling off of interest than by the breaking up of the large estates. Harvest-time still calls for a joyful celebration, but the large estates have been split and the units are smaller than in the days when the traditional harvest ceremonies were most fully observed.

The time when any farm operation begins, and the person who begins it, are always important. Great care is taken to avoid unlucky days and begin the harvest work on the day that is considered best for it. The Virgin's day, Saturday, is the luckiest of all. If it is not possible to begin the actual harvesting on a Saturday because of bad weather, because the grain is not ripe, or for any other reason, at least a few handfuls should be cut on that day.

Success may hinge also on choosing the right person to begin cutting, for the first shocks symbolically represent the whole harvest. In some places it may be a stranger, but he must be a good man for otherwise all the workers would cut themselves. Elsewhere the landlord himself must cut the first fistful of grain.

The ceremonious cutting of the first shocks may be the occasion of a minor feast—scrambled eggs, cheese and vodka brought out to the field. The owner of the land drinks to the leading harvester, and throws the remainder of his glass on the ground 'as an offering' to the ancestors, spirits and demons who inhabit the grain. On a large estate the head of the manor might hire a band and the harvest be begun to the strains of music.

Often the morning's work begins with a song. The leading girl harvester will sing:

Come out, young maiden
For the sun is risen
For the sun is on its way
Harvesters, be gay.

The ripe golden fields, changing colour in the sun, rising
and falling like waves of the sea, have brought out a wide
array of images and ideas. When the fields ripple in the
wind, people say 'the pigs are chasing one another', or
'sheep are walking on the grain'. One song sees a stag as the
animal moving the grain:

Gambol, gambol, oh stag
Over this lush barley
When the barley is gone
You will frolic no more.

But one must be careful in the ripe golden fields, for
dangerous beings move among the stalks. In many regions of
Poland children are warned of the wolf that lives in the
grain, and told that he will eat them if they walk there.
Pomeranians say the 'rye woman' or 'rye mother' lives in the
grain; the mountaineers speak of a black and naked 'wild old
woman' who lurks there. She seizes children and carries them
off to her underground home. Elsewhere are huge demons,
white robed and terrifying. Here and there they are pictured
as half woman, half animal, with the head of a frog, the
teeth of swine, the eyes of cows, and with claws on hands and
feet. The people of the Krakow region say these creatures are
women with flames shooting from their breasts.

There are also male grain demons, varying in different
places. One is an 'old man' who has three heads, each with
a long beard, and a fiery tail with which he smites children.
In order to placate the grain demons, the first handfuls of
grain cut are left as an offering.

The last blades cut during the harvest are treated with
elaborate ceremony. As the harvesters come to the end of the
cutting, they leave an armful of grain standing, and they

take care that it is the choicest. This remainder is then cut
with due ritual and flourish, and taken home. It is carefully
kept to be used in the next year's sowing, in order to assure
continuity and successful husbandry.

These last stalks are given various names by the farmers—
animal names for the most part, the two most common being
quail, and rabbit. These small creatures, particularly the
quail, make their home in the grain. Driven into smaller and
smaller areas as the harvesting progresses, they seek shelter
and are finally driven from the last sheaf.

The last remaining stalks of uncut grain are tied at the top
with a straw band, and all weeds are carefully removed. A
flat stone is placed in the centre and on it is placed bread,
sometimes with a pinch of salt and a coin as symbols of
human needs and assurance of abundance in the coming year.

When the 'quail' has been prepared, it must be 'ploughed
around'. The young men seize a girl who went out to do
harvest work for the first time that year, and drag her by the
feet around the standing sheaf, so that she may 'remember
for ever how to dress the quail'. This initiation of the novice is
less for her own sake than for increasing the fertility of the
fields during the next year.

Another name for the last sheaf, common not only in
Poland but also among other Slavic peoples, is *broda,* or
beard. In one region where this name is used, the leading
girl harvester thrusts a leafy branch of birch into the last
stalks of grain, binds them with a twig switch, rye and field
flowers. Around this 'beard' the male farmhands drag the
girl and as they do so sing a song beginning, 'Who does not
weed the beard will not live to see Sunday.'

Sometimes, too, the last sheaf cut assumes quasi-human
form and is called 'old woman' or 'old man'. It is put on a
wagon, with a stick thrust through it for arms, and is dressed
in the coat and hat of the owner of the land.

There are infinite local variations, but the basic pattern is everywhere the same: with music and song the last grains are brought ceremoniously to the cottage or manor house, later to be winnowed and used in the next spring's sowing. The leading girl and the leading man harvester play important parts in the ceremonies. They are chosen by common consent as the ones who stand out for ability and leadership in the work. Because of the ambivalent attitude toward leadership among the Poles, the harmonious acceptance of this role is interesting.

Perhaps the most beautiful songs of the harvest time are those sung by the harvesters as they leave the fields:

Fly not here, bright-winged falcon
For we'll come no more to this field
Fly not here, little wild quail
For we shall come here no more.

After the last sheaf has been brought home, comes the harvest celebration known as *wieniec*, wreath. Usually the 'wreath' or crown is made from the sheaf that has been brought in, brightly ornamented with flowers, red apples, and clusters of nuts. Occasionally stalks of oats and barley are added, clusters of mountain ash, or even a small wheaten loaf or gingerbread—in brief, an abundance of everything produced in the field, the orchard, the woods, and the apiary.

Fine grains in the wreath will bring a fine harvest the next year. In some places it is customary to steal the grain from the field of another, for the belief is widespread that another's grain will grow better than one's own.

The wreath is blessed in the church, sometimes a few days before the ceremony or even on the same day. Usually, however, the blessing is on the feast of the Assumption in celebration of Our Lady of the Herbs, when bouquets of herbs are also blessed. In some regions the master of the farm heads the

procession to the church for the blessing. Following him in a wagon drawn by four horses is the wreath, decorated with asparagus fern and paper bows.

In the ceremony proper, the wreath is worn by a girl, usually the leading girl harvester. It is an honour to be selected to wear it. It must be entrusted to a chaste girl, for one of less than perfect morals would bring poor harvest to the land.

The presentation of the wreath is the high spot of the harvest festival. It is accompanied by songs, all of which have certain common characteristics, in whatever part of the country they may originate. All express joy over the completed harvest, all sing praises and express respect and good wishes for the landowner and his family, often with extensive and highly flattering compliments:

> *Our master's stockyard is wide*
> *He has pretty daughters and*
> *Plenty of money.*

In the days of the large estates, the steward, who was seldom liked by the harvesters, was more apt to reap criticism or ridicule:

> *The drive is paved with flagstones gray*
> *The steward's legs are gray as they.*

The girl wearing the wreath leads the procession of harvesters, who sing a song such as the one quoted at the beginning of this section. As the procession approaches the farm cottage or manor house, it may receive a dousing of water, most of which goes to the leading girl and the leading man harvester—the *przodownica* and *przodownik*. This custom is a typical rain-charm, to insure good rainfall in the coming year. In some places the 'quail' or 'beard' is drenched for the same reason. Where people believe that the more water they pour, the more successful the harvest will be, the dousing may take violent form and even the master may not escape. One harvest song has this to say on the subject:

sentences, hinging mainly on reminiscences of the dead. All listen intently for signs that the guests have arrived. Every rustle, every creak or motion, is taken as evidence that they are entering.

Among the prescribed dishes for the feast are *kut ja*, a gruel of cooked wheat or barley eaten with honey; *bliny*, a kind of pancake; fruit and honey. The portions reserved for the dead are not touched by the living, and the fact that they appear to remain uneaten does not in the least affect the belief that the dead have feasted on them.

The reserved portions are never thrown away. Some may be put on the window sills for souls who come late, and some may be given to the beggars who wait for them outside the more prosperous houses. The portions reserved for the dead may also be given to the 'clean' beasts of the stables—horses, cattle, and sheep.

When the feast is over, the head of the house opens the door or window once more, and dismisses the guests with at least as much enthusiasm as his greeting conveyed. His words of farewell clearly reveal the hope that the entertainment offered has been sufficient to keep the invisible guests from returning very soon:

> *Sainted ancestors*
> *You came here to eat*
> *To eat—you have eaten*
> *To drink—you have drunk*
> *Homage and honour to you!*
> *Now tell us*
> *What do you need?*
> *Or better, go back to heaven*
> *Begone! Begone! Begone!*

WINTER IS A time for love, but it is not loved. It is the season of least work and also of least joy.

A great tedium hangs over the peasant's life during that season. The Polish winter is very hard; the snow is deep and communications are difficult. The days are short and no real outdoor work is possible. Time hangs heavy on everyone's hands.

This is the accepted season for courtship and marriage arrangements. It is felt that eligible young men and women really ought to get engaged during the period between St. Sylvester's (New Year's Eve) and Shrovetide. If they fail to do so they will suffer for it in the Shrovetide celebrations.

There are numerous social gatherings, too, some of them very gay—perhaps a spinning party where stories are told all night long, until dawn comes; perhaps an evening of singing and dancing. Moreover, some of the most rollicking holidays come in winter, furnishing a blessed break to monotony—and often a welcome end to a period of fasting. Nevertheless, the end of autumn is a melancholy time and the end of winter is a signal for rejoicing.

Although no regular outdoor work can be done, there are always farm chores to be carried on. The animals must be fed and tended. In bitter weather some of them are brought into the huts where they are hospitably sheltered by the already crowded family. The cow will be fastened in the passage way outside the main room, where she will have protection from the wind, but no additional warmth. If the family has a goat, that will be fastened nearby—though not too near. A baby calf would be taken in with the family, and made into a household pet. Chickens and hens would also be sheltered in   and lives.

They are   ftest and
warmest fee   animals.
Each anim   after the

health of the family, a news bulletin about the cow or horse will be included in the answer as a matter of course.

During the winter vegetables are dried, spinning is done, clothes and farm implements are made ready for the coming year. None of the tasks, however, and none of the pleasures can speed the winter months. They seem to crawl. It is dark and close in the huts, there are too many crowded into them —humans and animals. There is real hardship from cold, and sometimes from hunger. When spring comes again it feels like the start of a new life as well as of a new year.

The winter is ushered in by St. Martin, mounted on horse-back. If snow falls on his day, November 11, the saying goes that St. Martin arrived on a white horse, and a white winter is expected. If no snow has fallen, then St. Martin has come riding a black horse, and the winter will be mild.

St. Martin's has always been celebrated very gaily in Poland, as a final post-harvest flourish, before winter settles down in grim earnest. He is associated with the genial gods of plenty whose feasts had been celebrated at the turn of the season for centuries before his birth in 336 AD in a small Hungarian town. During his lifetime he was renowned as a great teacher and benefactor. In time, however, the learned and dignified saint came to be regarded as the patron of fields and meadows, of shepherds and flocks, and of birds—particularly of geese.

The goose appears beside St. Martin on headstones and old glass paintings and on early medieval calendars in West-ern Europe, and numerous legends seek to account for the connection. It is traditional to eat roast goose on his day— 'On St. Martin's the goose goes into the oven.'

The breastbone of the goose forecasts the weather of the coming winter. If it is white, the winter will be snowy and severe; if it is mottled, the weather will be changeable and uncertain:

For St. Martin's
To know what the winter will be
The goose is best
Look at the bone of her breast.

St. Martin's Eve provides one of several occasions for masked processions moving from house to house. Farmhands disguised in motley masquerade, with bells jingling about their necks, go from cottage to cottage, frightening and delighting the children. In this case, reversing the usual rule, it is the maskers who offer gifts to their audience—sweets, nuts, apples, pears. The children are told that St. Martin has sent them these presents.

On the eve of St. Martin's, some make a point of feeding the cattle smooth, straight straw so that they will look healthy and sleek when spring returns; and an onion to protect them from ticks. As for the winter crops—if they have not been sown by this time, small hope is held for them. The saying goes:

Gawel's oats, Martin's rye
Is worth about as much as a cat—or
The devil will take all.

St. Martin's day is one of unrestrained singing and dancing, of eating and drinking in abundance. Formerly the celebration would last several days, bringing together relatives, neighbours and friends. In addition to the proverbial goose, the feast would include roast veal, roast pork, roast chicken and sausage. The prosperous give to the poor so that they too might share the holiday cheer.

During the feast, St. Martin was toasted in the wine of the season and from this custom new wine came to be known as St. Martin's wine. Often too, in times past, they drank the health of the goose—a toast that presumably was seldom acknowledged.

In Poland, as throughout Western Europe, preparation of meat for winter food is begun on St. Martin's day—the slaughtering of cattle and fowl, to be smoked and salted.

From these activities the whole month used to be called *podgardle*, under the throat; and hogs were sometimes killed on St. Martin's for a feast known as *podgardle*.

Winter is the season of courting, and two holidays in late November are devoted to divinations by which young people try to discover whether, whom, and when they will marry. The boys try to read their future on St. Katherine's Eve, November 20. The girls still more elaborately make their divinations on the Eve of St. Andrew's, November 30. He is their special patron and girls eager to marry seek his help and protection through prayer, fasting and other mortification. The fasting encourages significant dreams—especially if at nightfall the girls eat herring to make them thirsty. Then at night their future husband will appear with water for them to drink.

Numerous methods of divination are used. One of the most common throughout Poland is the 'sowing' of hemp seeds, prepared on St. Katherine's Eve and kept since then. The girls carry the seed tied at their waists. Young men, who sometimes also 'sow the hemp seed', carry it in the right sleeve of their shirts.

Another general practice is making auguries from the shapes formed by pouring spoonfuls of melted wax on cold water. This custom is pictured in the opera *Straszny Dwor* by Moniuszko. The use of wax for divination or for black magic is among the oldest known, and is one strongly opposed by the church. An edict dated 1727 includes a proscription of the practice of pouring wax.

Another method used by the girls is to place their boots in order, in a line leading from the stove to the door. The girl whose boot is the first to come outside the door will be the first to marry. In still another, each girl prepares a tempting titbit for a dog. The dog is then brought in and the girl whose food he selects first, will be the first to marry.

Under certain circumstances, St. Andrew permits the girls to see their future mates while they are not dreaming. They may look into a mirror or a well to see the future spouse. Or as in one special variation, a girl may cook three vegetable dishes, lay the table for two, and say: 'In the name of the Father, the Son and the Holy Ghost, I bid thee to supper. Amen!' Thus commanded, the figure of the man is expected to materialize. It is considered advisable, however, not to put a knife on the table, for the vision might use it to inflict death.

The almost endless repertoire of divinations practised on St. Andrew's Eve are performed as a frolic, with much merry-making, and the loser is always marked as the one who will marry last.

St. Nicholas, viewed in general as a patron of cattle, horses and sheep, is specifically their protector against the wolf. His day, on December 6, is the particular holiday of shepherds and cowherds, and in many regions they fast on the Eve of St. Nicholas, to gain his good grace and protection. Some go so far as to carry offerings of fowl and hemp to church for him.

In hamlets and villages that are near dense forests, people have had to wage constant battle against marauding beasts, especially the wolf. They protected themselves by every means they could muster: dug huge pits at the edge of the forest, set traps and nets, staged frantic wolf hunts. All these were not enough, and the help of saints and of magic practices has constantly been invoked.

St. Nicholas was a likely protector of the flocks, famed for miraculous deeds performed during his life on earth and after his death. He is one of the heavenly hierarchy who has enjoyed equal veneration in the Eastern and Western churches.

The wolves do the saint's bidding, and will take only

those animals which he assigns to them. Otherwise all
livestock would become the prey of the wolves. He is always
just, both to the prey and the preyer. He keeps the wolf in
check and will not let him harm man too much; but he sees
that even the wild beast shall not starve. Because of his
divinely decreed jurisdiction over the wolves, when one of
them steals a sheep the owner may pray for its return in
these words:

> *Saint Nicholas*
> *Bring the keys from paradise*
> *And lock the wolf's jaw.*

It is said that the wolves meet at a certain spot on St.
Nicholas' Day and the saint tells each one what beast he
may seize in the coming year. A popular tale tells how a man
was punished for eavesdropping while these orders were
being given out. He wanted to find out if the saint really did
rule the wolves, so he hid in the branches of a pine tree on
St. Nicholas Day. The saint did indeed tell each beast in
turn what prey might seize. Coming finally to the last wolf, a
lame one, St. Nicholas ordered him to 'eat up the man who is
sitting in the pine tree'.

Terror-stricken, the man remained in the tree until
morning, then ran home and stayed in all the rest of the day.
Weeks later there was a knock at the door. Other members of
the family went in turn, and saw nothing. After repeated
knocking, the man went out, whereupon the wolf seized and
devoured him. Only his boots were left to bear testimony
that 'whatever is in the wolf's teeth was given him by St.
Nicholas'.

A similar role of master over the wolves and protector of
farm animals is often ascribed to St. George; and some of
the anecdotes told about St. Nicholas are told elsewhere
about St. George. Moreover, the winter St. Nicholas is
fused in the popular mind with the spring St. Nicholas,

actually a different and less important saint, whose day falls on May 9.

The autumn St. Nicholas, with the autumn St. George (November 25) and St. Barbara (December 4), helps to determine the character of the winter. If St. George covers the earth with a thick blanket of snow and St. Barbara then brings a thaw, followed by St. Nicholas bringing a hard frost, the winter will be a good one. From the standpoint of communication, a good freeze is much to be desired; it is also desirable for the winter grain which by now is in the ground.

If, contrary to what is expected of him, St. Nicholas brings a thaw, the winter will be changeable and the saint is reproached for having wet himself like a baby in the cradle. He is blamed even though it may have been one of the other saints who was remiss. Generally, however, St. Nicholas can be counted on to freeze the vegetables in the garden and the grain in the fields. 'There is no summer before the spring Saint Nicholas, no winter before the autumn one.'

That the colour of St. Martin's horse had already set the pattern for the winter, is merely another suggestion of the basis for frequent jurisdictional disputes among the saints.

The gift-bearing Santa Claus of western countries is hardly known as yet in Poland, although here and there the notion that St. Nicholas brings gifts at Christmas time has seeped in through foreign contact. In the cities, however, where fear of wolves does not exist, St. Nicholas appears as a kindly patron of good children, who makes his round on December 6, and has no connection with Christmas.

Parties in honour of the urban Saint Nicholas are among the most pleasant diversions of winter, and are known as *mikolajki*, or 'little nicholases'. The saint, impersonated by a tall man wearing a beard, cloak, and mitre, assisted by a

COLOURED PAPER CUT-OUTS TO ADORN WALL

THE TATRA MOUNTAINS

group of people in fantastic costumes, goes to the homes where parties are in progress and questions the children about their catechism. Correct answers are rewarded with sweets and toys; stupid ones with several lashes with a switch.

In art, as well as in folklore, the Polish St. Nicholas is always represented as a white-bearded, mitred bishop, tall and dignified. For Polish peasant children, however, his resemblance to Santa Claus stops with the beard.

As a religious festival, Christmas is second only to Easter in the hierarchy of holidays. As a gala time it ranks first of all. Like Easter, it is an extended celebration, for it continues from Christmas Eve to the Feast of Epiphany—known in Poland as the Feast of the Three Kings—on January 6. This two-week period holds some of the most colourful customs in all the treasury of Polish folklore.

The Christmas season in rural Poland does not come, as it does in an industrial and commercial society, at a period crowded with work and social activity. It offers a longed-for break in the frozen tedium of winter, and is awaited with an eagerness that builds up into excitement.

The Christmas celebration shows again the sense of unity and continuity in the peasant's life. Its homely dramatizations reveal how literally, concretely, and intimately he conceives the holy figures of his faith. An integral part of the religious ritual is the constant concern for the fertility and prosperity of the farms and the farmers—a concern often expressed in practices carried through from pre-Christian days.

The religious veneration for the holy period enhances peasant belief in its magical potency. Falling at the time of the winter solstice, when 'day is but a short twilight twixt night and night', this is a period of wondrous and uncanny happenings. Water in the springs and streams changes into

G

wine and honey on Christmas Eve. If one who is pure of heart draws a pitcher of this water he will be rich and happy all through his life. On this, as on other special nights, the waters also become magically healing. The afflicted make pilgrimages to frozen rivers and lakes in the conviction that if they dip the affected parts while the bells peal for midnight mass, they will be cured.

In barns and stables the animals talk to each other in human voices that only the innocent can safely comprehend. Bells submerged at the bottom of frozen lakes moan in hollow tones. Popular legend has preserved dreadful tales of bold ones swallowed up by streams from which they had sought to draw the magic wine, or of the farmer who heard his own death sentence from the mouths of his own oxen when he eavesdropped on their talk.

By his behaviour during this time a person can assure himself a good year. Many of the practices are designed to propitiate spirits and agents that may work harm to husbandry, and to invoke help and protection for the crops. It is also a time to find out, by divination and augury, what is in store for the crops and for one's personal fortunes. And it is one of the periods when the dead mingle with the living. The very fervour of its religious tone activates beliefs and practices associated with the ancestor worship that the church has tried to discourage.

Preparation for the Christmas holidays, as for many others, is part of the joy they bring. It begins early in Advent and offers one of the chief diversions for the young people during long winter evenings. While the men and boys are contriving wonders for the outdoor festivities, the girls work on ornaments to give the cottage a holiday dress and to trim the tree which will occupy the place of honour.

As in all Western Christendom, the tree is one of the high spots of the festivities, especially for the children. It is trimmed

much like Christmas trees in other countries, with paper chains, apples and nuts wrapped in gold or silver foil, ginger-bread figures, multi-coloured ribbons, paper flowers, and gay ornaments of paper or beads.

On the tree may be hung also *swiaty*—'worlds' or 'spheres' —about the size of an orange, made from coloured Christmas wafers. The organist bakes these wafers, paper-thin like the Communion wafer but larger, square or rectangular, and impressed with the holy symbols. Early in Advent he takes a package of wafers to every household in the village. Then the father or mother will send one of them to every member of the family who is away from home, in time to reach him for Christmas. Wafers may also be sent to cherished friends. If the family is one of high standing in the parish, the package of wafers will be large; and if there is a nimble-fingered girl in the family, she will fashion some of them into the coloured *swiaty* for the tree. Or one may be hung from the ceiling, where it will remain for the whole year. Nor does the work of the organist go unrewarded, for he is well paid with gifts. As a sub-functionary of the church—less than a priest but more than a peasant—he is constantly performing semi-secular functions for which he receives constant and concrete recognition.

The tree itself is called *podlaznik, podlazniczka, podlisnizka,* or simply *sad*—orchard. It may be a whole evergreen tree, a section of one, or merely a large branch. In any case the Poles have their own way of placing it—it is hung point down from the ceiling, in the principal corner of the room or over the table where the Christmas feast is spread.

The girls make other decorations also, in the dimly lit cottages during the nights before Christmas. Paper cutouts are prepared, to be used as a frieze on the walls or as a border around the table-cloth. Chandelier-like ornaments are fashioned of coloured paper and straw, to be hung from the

ceiling. These are known as *pajaki*, spiders, because some oɪ
them have the spreading effect of a spiderweb. Other
materials may be introduced—wire or string to make the
spreading strands, feathers and beads to add variety. The
'spider' may be just a 'star'—small and round—or it may ray
out like the web that gave it its name, bestrewn with cutouts,
feathers, paper flowers or geometrical designs. The spiders
are among the most characteristic decorations of the Polish
peasant's home. They may hang from the ceiling all the year
round, although they soon become darkened with smoke. For
each new season, new *pajaki* may be evolved.

In making the gay and elaborate cutouts, paper is first
folded and cut for the basic pattern. Then other colours are
pasted on with egg-white, flour and water, or paste that has
been bought. Repeated pasting, folding and cutting produces
works of amazing ingenuity and variety, for the Polish
peasant is an artist with paper and shears. Each region has
its own style, but within that style each individual exercises
his own talents, striving for something new, different,
delightful. On occasion, unbelievably complicated lacy
designs are produced with sheep-shears. Some look as if they
were made of wire rather than paper, and to the dexterity of
form is added the invention of adroit colour combination.
Different shades are applied where even the basic form seems
too fine-drawn for paper and shears to achieve.

The pictures are always strictly stylized, avoiding any
naturalistic appearance. The geometrical designs include
circles, ovals, and often very long rectangles, the composition
of which can be reduced to a few variants. There are
geometric or plant designs based on a symmetrical arrangement of rings, or rooster and peacock motifs worked out
around a common axis. There is also a characteristic variant
employing stylized human figures: weddings, field work,
scenes from religious life.

Christmas is enjoyed not only as a break in the winter dullness but also as an end to a long period of strict fasting. The Polish peasant is both devout and poor. Since he will not eat meat during the six weeks before Christmas, and has little palatable food in its stead, the time is one of real deprivation.

Preparation of the Christmas fare takes many days and reaches its climax during the last week of Advent. The important meal of the holidays is *wigilia*, Christmas Eve supper. As it falls within the period of fasting, *wigilia* is meatless— *postnik*—but it is none the less opulent. Even if the family is poor, this meal and the Easter feast are prepared without thought of economy.

Tradition prescribes the number of dishes that should be included in the meal. In some localities it is nine, in others eleven—but always an odd number, to allow for the possibility of increase. Even numbers are looked on as conclusive.

One requirement for the Christmas Eve menu is common to all localities: all the dishes served should represent the produce of the farmer's land and industry, and all the sources of his produce should be represented. Most often there are mushrooms for the woods, wheat or millet for the field, dried pears or prunes for the orchard, peas and cabbage for the kitchen garden, and, where fish is eaten, herring to represent the waters.

The great care with which the peasant manages to have all his food sources represented in the significant Christmas meal reflects his belief in the symbolic influence of such representation for perpetuating his food supply. It also reflects the tendency to personify everything about him. The woods, the fields, the waters are sensate entities, responsive to gratitude but ready to rear up in anger and withhold their gifts if they fail to receive their due.

The various foods are combined in many different dishes throughout the country, but certain ones are found almost

everywhere. One of these is poppy-seed cake. The dough is the usual cake dough made with yeast, sugar, eggs, and butter—or, in the more frugal households, flax-seed oil. The filling is made of ground poppy-seed, raisins, egg, sugar or a little honey, and a dash of cinnamon and rum if they are on hand. The dough is flattened out quite thin, spread with the poppy-seed paste, rolled, glazed with white of egg, and baked in large enough quantities to last through the holidays.

Also widely served in peasant homes is the *kutja,* made of cracked wheat or barley, poppy seed, honey and milk, mixed to the consistency of a thin porridge. It is eaten as a sweet at the end of the meal and can be very palatable.

Other common dishes are prune or poppy-seed *pierogi,* resembling strudels, cabbage with peas, and mushroom soup. In the cities, marinated herring, fish in aspic, and a fish broth thickened with sour cream and served with noodles are regular seasonal dishes. The common 'sweet' at the end of the city meal is a compote of stewed dried fruits.

As Christmas Eve approaches, the bustle in the house reaches fever-pitch. The interior, already thoroughly cleaned and scrubbed, is given a final going over. The freshly scoured furniture is put in place, the paper cutouts are hung on the walls and from the ceiling, the Christmas tree is trimmed and hung where tradition or the taste of the family dictate. Straw is spread over all the floors, and a sheaf of each of the four principal grains—wheat, rye, oats and barley—is placed in the four corners of the room. The thought behind this practice is the same as that which dictates representing the chief food sources in the Christmas feast.

The table is laid in a special way. To commemorate Christ's birth in a manger, hay is spread over the tabletop, to lie beneath the cloth. In the country a whole sheaf is used, but in city homes a few symbolic blades suffice. The housewife's best linen is used, and the table must be set for an even

number of people. Otherwise one will die during the coming year.

An extra place is set for a possible guest or beggar as none must be turned away on this sacred night. 'God enters the home when a guest enters in', or 'A guest in the house is God in the house' are popular sayings all over Poland on Christmas Eve. In some places the belief is strong that it is good luck to entertain a guest on this night. Guests are customarily treated with great honour in Polish peasant homes, but dining out is little encouraged except on special occasions such as this.

Frequently a place is also set at the table for a recently deceased member of the family, since this is one of the times when the dead return to earth. There is an almost universal belief that graves open on Christmas Eve, allowing ghosts and spirits to wander on the earth until the Feast of the Three Kings. Because there are so many more people dead than living, the peasant imagines the dead as fairly swarming in his very home.

On this, as on all occasions, he does his utmost to show them the respect that will win their favour and protect him against the disaster that offence to them might bring. He will blow on the bench before sitting down to the Christmas feast, in order not to crush a soul that might be sitting there. He may walk warily for fear of stepping on an invisible guest, and take care not to spill water for fear of wetting one. Certain kinds of work are avoided throughout the holidays, especially after sunset. For example, one must not spin or twist anything for fear of entangling a wanderer who would surely take vengeance for the disrespect. Even if one is less certain than his grandfather was that the air is literally alive with disembodied souls, it is practical as well as traditional to show respect for beings whose non-existence has after all not been proved.

With the table laid, the food ready, the family resplendent in their best clothes, the room takes on an air of hushed expectancy. The children are at the windows, or outdoors if the day is mild enough, waiting for the first star to appear. For, in commemoration of the star of Bethlehem, the appearance of the first star on Christmas Eve is the long awaited sign for the festivities to begin.

This moment is awaited eagerly on more than religious grounds. The last day's fast is rigorous everywhere. In many households, especially in Silesia, nothing is eaten on this last day but a crust of bread taken with a little water in the morning—a custom often observed before a fast-breaking feast. There is good reason for all to be famished at this moment and the children, most anxious and most famished of all, watch the skies tensely, each hoping to be the first to cry out, 'The star!' So important is the star that it has given its name to the occasion. The formal name of the holiday is *Boze Narodzenie*, the Nativity; but the popular, everyday term, the one used by children and by adults in ordinary conversation is *Gwiazdka*, Little Star.

As soon as the star appears all exchange greetings, offer blessings and good wishes to each other. Then at last they sit down to supper, breaking the long fast with gusto. In most peasant homes the food is all placed on the table at one time, usually before the family sits down. The one exception is the sweet *kutja*, which is brought in at the very end.

The first part of the meal passes in silence. Everyone is too hungry to do anything but eat—slowly always, and with decorum, but with utter concentration. After the first hunger is appeased, the solemn mood relaxes. But through all, no matter how gay the mood, runs a concern for the crops and for good fortune in the year to come. The meal itself may be punctuated by observances that brighten the

even throw handfuls of oats and barley back at the priest when he sprinkles them. The observance is an ancient one and can easily be traced to various customs of throwing grain, bread, or money on people as a magical device to insure fertility, success, beauty, and plenty. But the peasants explain the throwing of grain on their neighbours or on the priest as a reminder of the martyrdom of St. Stephen, who was stoned to death.

Another, and very important, custom is connected with December 26. This is the traditional day when all work agreements are concluded and the farmhand is either re-hired for another year by his employer, or leaves to seek other employment. Now that the large estates have been broken down, the custom is gradually declining, but the old saying related to it is still popular:

On St. Stephen's day, servants go their way
On St. Stephen's, man and master are even
On St. Stephen's day, every man is (his own) master.

In the old days, farmhands would gather at the tavern on St. Stephen's, and a collective process of individual bargaining was carried on. The men gave their verdict on their employers, while the employers by standing drinks and offering attractive terms tried to secure the services of the best farmhands.

In some villages the housewife would prepare an especially good meal for St. Stephen's. If a workman accepted the master's invitation to sit down at the table and join the family in the meal, it was a sign that he would accept employment for another year. If he refused, and left the room, he thereby gave notice that he was leaving his employer's service. The neighbours would ask who did not 'eat the *barszcz*' and then make their offers to the man.

The twelve nights between Christmas and Epiphany are called *Swiete Wieczory*, the Holy Evenings. Carols are sung in the family circle during this time, and certain kinds of work

H

are prohibited. The period is special, not only because of the belief that spirits wander the earth during the Holy Evening. In some regions it is also believed that any work done after sunset will invite wolves, and that shaking anything will influence the behaviour of any being born during this time—the new born will shake as the object shook. In others, woodchopping is forbidden, for fear it might maim the unborn.

The twelve evenings are also thought to represent the twelve months of the year. People can forecast the weather for each of the next twelve months by the weather that prevails on its symbolic representative during the Holy Evenings. The Evenings are held in awe for still another reason. It is believed that God Himself walks the earth during this time, keenly watching the observance of all the precepts laid down for those who inhabit it.

Before the Holy Evenings end, with the Feast of the Three Kings on January 6, the new year has begun. It slips in quietly, ushered by St. Sylvester's on December 31—for as has been noted, the peasant's year really begins with the spring. December 31 is known as St. Sylvester's, and seldom as New Year's Eve. It is not a folk holiday, although it is celebrated in the cities. New Year's Day is also little celebrated, although girls sometimes make divinations with little figures, as on St. Andrew's day, to find out what their future husbands will be like.

As in all Christendom the Purification on February 2 is Candlemas Day, known in Poland as Our Lady of the Candles. Women, and some of the men, take candles to church on that day and have them blessed during the service. The ceremony ends with a procession around the church, in which the lighted candles are carried. This is a tense and breathless procedure, for if a candle goes out when there is no wind, during the procession or on the way home, it is considered a bad omen.

After the lighted candle has been brought home, a cross is sometimes burned with it on the central beam of the ceiling, to guard against lightning and to bring good fortune. The farmer makes a tour of all his buildings with the lighted candle, so that the magic of the blessed flame will radiate over his farm. When it has been extinguished, the smoke is inhaled as protection against sore throat. The candle may then be placed on the wall over the head of a bed and kept there for the whole year to remind the occupants that they must live in preparation for the life to come. It is lighted on solemn occasions. For example, the lighted candle is put in the hands of the dying to lessen the agony of death and ward off evil spirits. During storms, it may be lighted and put on the window sill.

Among the rhymed saying about Candlemas are: 'If it is dripping from the roof on Candlemas, that year the *leniec* will shine'—that is, the flax will come in wild; 'If there is a thaw on Candlemas, the harvests will be thin'; 'If the roof is dripping on Candlemas, the winter will hold yet a while'.

As in many places, the peasants believe that unseasonable warmth on February 2 bodes no good.

A Candlemas saying in another sphere is, 'On Our Lady of the Candles, adieu my handsome one'. This was said about suitors who had failed to propose by that day, leaving too little time for them to marry before Lent. It again brings out the importance attached to winter as a mating season. In this frozen interim of nature, human beings like the fields, the orchards and the woods, should be mobilizing their energies for new life.

IV THE PARTS OF THE WHOLE

Each village has a different song
Each country has a different custom
Each house has its own morals
Each home has its own rules.

THE UNIT THAT is Poland falls into distinct parts, each with characteristics that set it off from the others. These parts in turn show subdivisions—small districts that contrast with the surrounding area. Whatever generalizations are made about Poles and Polish life—and a good many can be made—the numerous regional and local differences must be recognized.

The parts may be variously defined, according to the angle from which they are viewed. One sweeping distinction is between urban and rural Poland. In many respects, the towns and cities throughout the country have more in common with each other than each urban centre has with its immediate rural environs. Costumes, customs, the assumptions on which behaviour is based, the tempo and tone of daily life in Warsaw would resemble those of Krakow more than those of the nearest villages.

The speech of the city, for example, is easily distinguishable from that of the country. Each geographical region has its own characteristic dialect, pronunciation and intonation. Yet in any region it is possible to recognize instantly whether the speech is that of the town or of the country. A peasant who goes to the university, enters an urban calling, and becomes 'citified' must change his speech. Although traces of the village dialect often remain in it to the end of his days, he can usually modify the more obvious features—for example, the peasant tendency to say h for g, k for x, or z for zh.

The content as well as the form of his speech will change. He will probably draw less frequently on the rich store of rhymed proverbs that are a correct and almost a required part of rural discourse. He will try to speak less slowly than the measured delivery which the peasant considers dignified and proper. He will cultivate also at least an appearance of greater spontaneity and less exaggerated reserve.

Since the present account is concerned only with the Polish peasants, the overall contrast between town and country will be assumed rather than discussed in detail. It may be assumed also that some of the characteristics of the various regions are visible in the towns and cities that lie within them.

Aside from the urban-rural distinction, there are definite regional differences apparent among the peasants in various parts of Poland. The products of history and of geography, they contribute much to the colour and flavour of Polish peasant life.

The regions defined by differences in peasant ways and habits are not official and absolute. They do not necessarily correspond with formal administrative units, though their existence has been reflected in governmental machinery. They exist chiefly in the minds and lives of people rather than on paper. They cannot be represented by clear-cut boundary lines because each fades gradually into its neighbour. Yet there is general agreement on the end of one and the beginning of the next. The inhabitants of each are recognized by signs so familiar that they seldom provoke comment. Common assumptions exist about the characteristics of the natives of each region.

In the Poland of today there are six major regions, each with smaller subdivisions displaying local customs and special traits. Although they are recognized, accepted, and constantly referred to, these regions are not commonly given formal definition in published maps. They are:

Mazowsze—Mazovia—lying in the centre of Poland
Malopolska—Little Poland—on the upper Vistula
Wielkopolska—Great Poland—on the middle Oder and Warta
Pomorze—Pomerania—on the shore of the Baltic Sea
Slask—Silesia—on the upper Oder
Podhale—the Carpathian and sub-Carpathian area

Unofficial as the regional divisions of Poland may be, they are firmly rooted in history. The ethnic groups that form the core of each one have retained their identities and their approximate locations throughout ten centuries. A map of the tribes occupying this territory a thousand years ago corresponds roughly to the present 'culture areas'.

The contrast between regions has been heightened by more recent influences. For many years Poland was divided between Germany, Austria, and Russia, and each of these countries subordinated the economic and cultural development of the areas under its control to its own interests. The portions under German sway, for example, became more highly industrialized than the others, developed better schoois and better roads.

Differences in regional style are evident in the traditional designs and patterns employed for decoration. The colours and motifs used for embroidery, pottery, textile design and paper cut outs show marked regional characteristics. Within each region there are also strong local variations. Moreover, within the limits of each style there is always room for the individual virtuosity and originality so highly prized by Polish peasants.

Similar regional differences are found in music and in dance, which are inseparable. They are also found in the folklore. Not only are specific tales or songs different from one region to another, but the characteristic themes vary— always within the limits of the over-all national character.

In one place there are ballads but no epics; in another, the Cinderella theme is prominent, and little is heard about historic exploits.

The appearance of the peasant cottages again shows the regional influence, although the basic ground-plan is similar throughout the country. The exterior may be white-washed, washed in tints of blue, orange, decorated with designs, or left unpainted; or it may be white with bright red window frames, delightful against the green of the orchard. The roof may be thatched or shingled, or even made of woven slats, with its shape varying according to the dictates of the material and of local tradition.

Even the layout of the village varies regionally. When peasants were transferred from the eastern region to the newly acquired territory in the west, they startled their new neighbours by promptly reproducing the ground plan of their native villages, which was quite unlike the one familiar in the territory to which they were moved.

One of the most obvious and easily recognized marks of regional difference is clothing, for each region has its distinctive style and there are many local variations within each one. At the same time there are constants which appear in the costume of any Polish peasant.

The typical peasant woman in any region will wear a 'shirt', which is a combination blouse and petticoat. She will wear over it a full skirt, perhaps a bodice or jacket, and probably a kerchief or head-covering of some sort, especially if she is married. If she is married, however, it would be a cap and not one of the eleaborate head-dresses that are the delight of the Polish girl. An amazing variety of materials may be combined in these head-dresses which at times reach startling heights: flowers, feathers, beads, ribbons, tinsel, metal ornaments, stiffened muslin, are built and wired into structures that to western eyes sometimes appear fantastic.

Young girls may also wear their hair uncovered or adorned with a wreath or flower.

The headgear is highly important and even the simple kerchief allows for infinite ingenuity in the way it is tied and arranged. Important also are the ornaments and necklaces without which no dress costume is complete. The shape and substance of the ornaments conform to regional patterns, but profusenesss of ornamentation is a costume constant.

The indispensable apron, even more than the headgear, is something beyond mere apparel. It can be used as a kerchief to cover the head, as a shawl, or as a container for carrying things. It can also be used to convey a mood or a message, since it furnishes opportunity for elaborate play without words. A girl twists one corner to register shyness, flips her apron in coyness, throws it over her head in embarrassment, or in an excess of modesty while she accepts a sip of vodka. An integral part of the costume, for dress as well as for workaday wear, it finds an infinite number of shapes, colours, decorations. A clean apron on Sunday, and a fancy one, is almost an essential to piety.

The men are nearly as much addicted to spectacular headgear as the women. In general the rule for both sexes seems to be, the more you can pile on your head the better. Like the girls, the men are ready to flaunt feathers, ribbons, beads and shells—though flowers are not relished as masculine adornment.

One difference between country and city is that the peasant tucks his trousers inside his boots—except for the mocassin-wearing mountaineers. The trousers vary in shape, growing narrower as one approaches the mountains and spreading to pantaloons in some parts of the lowlands. The men wear a variety of belts, some very wide, some heavily encrusted with metal.

Although colour preference is one index of locality, there

is an over-all fondness for the national colours, red and white. 'What is red is beautiful', they say. Traditional imagery in poetry speaks of the red kerchiefs or skirts of the peasant women gleaming across the fields.

Whatever the colour, if it is one of the real peasant fabrics, it will not fade. Woven of wool, flax or hemp, often on the peasant's own loom, the textiles made into the traditional folk costumes are good to last for twenty years. Work clothes may be made of cheap fabric bought at the fairs, but the traditional peasant costume, now worn chiefly for dress, is made to endure.

An intangible constant in Polish peasant attire is the love of finery and the great pride in the traditional costume. Men and women love to dress in their best, and grasp any opportunity to do so. Every holiday, every family celebration, every trip to the fair, every Sunday is an occasion for dressing up. All these occasions are enjoyed in part because they give one an opportunity to put on best clothes and play the peacock.

Perhaps no feature of the costume itself is as striking as the peasant's pride in it and admiration of it. In line with his prevailing attitude toward city life and people, there is no feeling of inferiority about urban costume. On the contrary, city clothes are scorned. If the peasant does discard his own and adopt city dress it is as a rule for strictly practical reasons, and with regret.

An incident during the Russian occupation of 1941 illustrates the love of finery and also the note of apparent incongruity that sometimes bewilders an outsider. Some Russian soldiers came into a village on a Sunday and saw the peasants dressed for church. 'Aha,' they exclaimed, 'you are the rich landowners', and were for seizing them all. The peasants insisted that they were not rich but were terribly poor and oppressed. It was hard to convince the Russians that these grandly dressed villagers were in fact the oppressed, toil-ridden victims to whom the sympathy of fellow workers was due.

Mazovia occupies part of the great central plain, in the basin of the middle Vistula and its tributaries, an area with many lakes. Its main city, Warsaw, has been the capital of Poland since the end of the sixteenth century, when it was chosen because of its central geographical position to succeed Krakow.

The people of Mazovia are called the Mazurs, and although its soil is mostly sandy, barren and unproductive, the majority of them are engaged in agriculture. The Mazurs are generally considered to be hardworking, thrifty, stubborn and conservative. Among some of the educated urban Poles it is also said that they are thrifty, ignorant and crude—perhaps because their stiff-necked insistence on political rights and prerogatives in earlier times set up an irritation that has persisted.

Their speech, even more than that of most Polish peasants, is slow, deliberate, and studded with proverbs. It is also witty and to the point. In all these characteristics it merely differs in degree from that of Polish peasants in general. They are apt to speak with great deliberateness and caution, but what they say is pithy and often colourful. And though their expressions are guarded and highly formalized, with all deference to the rules, they are seldom timid about expressing their convictions and demanding their due. The slow and cautious speech is linked with the peasant's emphasis on dignity and decorum. When they are talking to strangers, especially to city folk, suspicion exaggerates the deliberateness of their customary tempo. This habit of slow speech has contributed to the city-dwellers habitually considering the peasant as slow-witted. But the urban scoffers are mistaken. Whatever his verbal style, the average peasant is not stupid.

Mazovia is the region where struggle for land is most severe and where the tradition of farmer 'abdication' is most strong—as is natural since it is among the most populous and least fertile parts of Poland. Educationally and economically it is backward. Its schools have a low standing, its illiteracy rate is high compared to some other parts of the country; and at least until the second World War, none of its cities except Warsaw had a modern sewage system.

Nevertheless, it has more industrial centres than most of the other regions, and industrialization is increasing. Lodz, Zyrardow and Tomaszow are outstanding textile manufacturing towns. The development of industrial activity and of large manufacturing centres has created a large working-class quite different from the rural population in concepts, language and manners.

Warsaw itself is not only the capital of Poland, but also the great centre of learning. Here are located the largest and the most important institutions of scientific, industrial and medical research. And here, accordingly, are gathered the largest number of learned men and students. Yet, though Warsaw is the centre of learning, it has not wrested from historic Krakow the title of culture-centre. Progress, power and potential are in Warsaw, but the glamour and the legendary aura cling to the picturesque battlements of the southern city.

The folklore of Mazovia is more limited and less colourful than that found in some other regions. Much of it features the Cinderella theme, with emphasis on the punishment of the stepmother rather than on the future happiness of Cinderella. The motif of the brother who defends his sister from a cruel husband is also prominent. There are no historical songs even of local heroes, and no epics.

If the Mazur represents the epitome of peasant stubbornness, conservatism, and restraint, he is also typical in the element of underlying fire. For Mazovia is the home of the Mazurka, best loved of Polish dances, and one of the most spirited. The themes of Chopin's mazurkas were taken from Mazovia, and the native Mazur is recognized as the master performer of the dance.

Just as the dour Mazur has his bursts of flame, so the region itself has splashes of local colour. One is the famous shrine of the Black Madonna in Czestochowa, which draws great throngs of pilgrims every year. The typical costume of the men near Czestochowa includes a deep blue jacket contrasting with the coral stripes of the trousers, and a high, cone-shaped hat.

The most vivid spot in Mazovia is the neighbourhood surrounding the town of Lowicz. For many centuries the Lowicz area was owned by the Archbishops of Gniezno and it has maintained its individual characteristics even though it ceased long ago to be a separate principality. Except for the mountain region, Lowicz is the area most distinguished for exuberance in costume and in decorations. Its superb paper cut-outs are famous, as are the gay, almost gaudy costumes of its people. The most famous wool fabrics come from the neighbourhood of Lowicz, where rainbow-coloured stripes are especially popular. Stripes are well liked through-out Poland and local varieties are recognized by their characteristic width, spacing and colour. But nowhere are stripes so prevalent as in Lowicz. They are used for men's trousers, for the women's aprons, and especially for their skirts.

Like most Polish peasants, the men tuck their full, gaily striped trousers into high boots. They wear either a short black sleeveless jacket, a black cape or a long white coat, and stiff black hats trimmed with gold braid.

The women's costumes are even more resplendent, curiously combining stripes with lace designs. The skirts are striped in red, yellow, green and orange and are stiffly lined, gathered, and flounced out by several petticoats so that a woman of Lowicz in full dress regalia commands an impressive amount of space. Often the apron, lavishly trimmed with braid, is made of matching fabric; or it may be white, embroidered with flowers. Bodices of coloured velvet, richly embroidered, cover white linen blouses with puffed, lace-trimmed sleeves. Bead necklaces, and coral and silver ornaments tied with coloured ribbons are especially numerous.

Head kerchiefs are bright and the women's headdresses even more ornate and amazing than usual. Some tower two feet above the wearer's forehead. A bride of Lowicz usually wears on her head a veritable monument to human ingenuity in her majestic wedding crown of stiffened muslin, tinsel and flowers. Even the married women reconcile the dictates of decorum and of fancy in enormous ballooning caps of stiffened batiste.

In most of Mazovia, colours are more subdued than in Lowicz. Near Warsaw the men wear a dark-blue greatcoat brightened by fuchsia-coloured lapels and a variegated woollen sash ending in long tassels. People from Kujawy neighbourhood are popularly called 'Blue Patches' because they use so much dark blue. The men's greatcoats are of this deep blue shade, with long collars covering their shoulders like a cape. Their stiff hats have high crowns, flat straight brims, and a burst of decoration at some point. A feature of weddings in the Kujawy region is a dance performed solemnly while balancing a full glass on the brim of the hat. The glass is emptied only after the dance is done.

In Kurpie, colours are still more subdued. Grey is predominant in the men's attire, but contrast is added by deep blue lapels, red belt and peacock feathers tucked into the hat. The women wear dark, even black skirts. But their bodices or ornate boleros introduce colours, as do the 'shirts' embroidered in red. The most striking feature of the girls' costume in the Kurpie district is the headdress of black velvet, tall and cylindrical like a drum major's hat, with a large bunch of flowers or feathers at the side.

Only the western section of Little Poland is part of the country today. The eastern and larger portion has been made over to Russia. Krakow, the great centre of Little Poland, is the former capital—and even today in a sense the cultural capital—of Poland. One of Europe's oldest universities, founded in 1364, is in Krakow, and there also is the Polish Academy of Arts and Sciences. The history of Polish culture was in large measure shaped by men of Krakow. Today it is the area of most urbanity and greatest culture. The appearance of the city matches its role, for it is magnificent and monumental, with many Renaissance and Gothic churches, and one of the most beautiful royal castles in the world.

Because the city is large and the region small, Krakow dominates a considerable portion of Little Poland, and when one speaks of Krakovians one means not only the inhabitants of the city but those of its environs, including a substantial portion of those who are native to Little Poland.

The typical Krakovian is popularly conceived as far more sunny and vivacious than the typical Mazur. Their music is gay, their dances bouncing. To their neighbours they seem remarkably carefree, so that it is said the Krakovians like their week to be made of three work days and four days of rest.

Of all the Polish folk-costumes, the Krakovian is considered the most representative. If a Pole has to describe the national costume, he would be apt to describe this one, and with reason, for the famous coat of the Hussars comes from Krakow, as does the army hat. To foreigners, the Krakovian version has represented the typical Polish costume—in old Dutch and Flemish paintings a foreign or exotic figure was apt to be pictured in the flaring red coat of the Hussar.

The national colours, white and red, are those most in evidence among the Krakovians; but the red in this region verges on fuchsia, and this is the shade of the Hussar coat. It is called *amarant*. As one travels southward the overcoats grow shorter and the trousers more full and pantaloon-like. A popular cloak for men is the white *sukmana*, with a wide *amarant* hem and a very broad collar, drooping to a point at the back and stiff with glittering embroidery.

The Krakovians are particularly fond of ornamental belts. Some are very wide, thickly studded with brass; others are narrow, with dangling brass rings.

The square-cornered hat worn by the men is much like the Polish student caps seen in academic campus processions, except that it is adorned with a tall tuft of peacock feathers and a cluster of ribbon streamers. In its army version it is worn without ribbons and feathers.

The Krakovian women, like their sisters in Lowicz, outdo the men in the rich ornamentation of their costumes. Embroidery is extremely handsome, often done in white on white, with many openwork designs for blouses, caps, aprons, kerchiefs. The full trousers worn by the men look almost scanty against the billowing skirts of the women, starched, and gay with flower designs. Sumptuous bodices, gleaming with silver or gold embroidery, add to the carnival of colour. Multiple strands of coral beads are fastened at the back with vari-coloured ribbons that stream and flutter down to the edge of the skirt. And to enhance the rainbow effect, the bright red boots may be laced with green.

Great Poland, north of Little Poland and west of Mazovia, is considered the cradle of the Polish state. Its chief towns, Gniezno and Poznan, are the oldest in Poland, and Poznan was the first capital, before Krakow. Poland's oldest cathedral is in Gniezno.

As part of the Polish plain, the landscape of Great Poland, is level but never monotonous. The countryside is broken up by innumerable small lakes, most of them sausage shaped. The marshy plains bordering all the rivers have been reclaimed by a system of canals, and intensive cultivation of the land has made this area one of the country's largest grain producers, even though its soil is not fertile.

Industrialization is progressing, however. While peasant farms still dominate the landscape, towns are growing more numerous and larger, developing milling, brewing, sugar refining, paper making and the manufacture of agricultural machinery.

Like all western and central Poland, Great Poland is thickly settled. Unlike its neighbour, Mazovia, it came under German influence. Accordingly it has excellent roads, perhaps the best in Poland, its schools are many, good, and well attended, and its general standard of living is above the average for Poland.

Its chief city, Poznan, may be somewhat prosaic compared to Krakow and Warsaw, but Poznan has its own beauties and traditions, going back to the eleventh century when Poland's first kings set up residence there. According to legend, those first kings—of the Piast dynasty—were chosen from among the peasantry by two emissaries from God, because there was no virtue among the nobility.

Legend also tells that Poznan and Gniezno were founded by three brothers, Lech, Czech, and Russ, who lived in the land between the Baltic and the Black Sea, the Oder and the Dniester. After their father died, the three brothers separated and each went out to wander the world. But all were homesick and after many years, by a miracle, all came home on the same day. They met on a road and although they were so much older, they knew one another at once. They wept for joy, crying out *'Poznaje!'*—'I know you!' And on the place where they met, they built the city of Poznan, where the River Chybin flows into the Wartha.

But the three brothers did not remain together. Czech went to the West, where he founded the Czech nation; Russ to the East, where he founded the Russian nation; while Lech stayed by the River Wartha and founded Poland. On his excursions throughout the country, he discovered in the forest a very beautiful green valley bordered by high trees. Lech decided to build a city in that spot, and ordered the trees felled. When the men cut down the biggest tree, a swarm of white eagles which had nested in it flew up to the sky. Lech was so overwhelmed by the magnificence of the sight that he named the city Gniezno, or nest, and made the white eagle Poland's national emblem. One of the many tales told about Gniezno is that it was the first home of Krakus, who founded Krakow.

The cradle of the Polish state is also the birthplace of the polonaise, one of Poland's oldest dances, and one that has lent its form to concert stage as well as to ballroom. At one time the polonaise was used to open balls all over Europe. Formerly a dance of the nobility, today it survives chiefly in Great Poland, where it is also called 'slow dance' or 'marching dance'. In fact it differs little from a stylized and much elaborated march.

Its music has a rhythm of three long quarter notes to the measure and usually consists of two parts of six, eight or ten measures. The dance movements emphasize the second beat and step of the measure, a nicety few foreigners understand.

At first only men danced the polonaise, but before it swept through other lands women also were included. As an old Polish dance of knighthood, it was performed in the rich costume of the nobility with sword at side, and at appropriate moments the sword was drawn with a flourish or the plumed hats swept off in a lordly bow.

I

The polonaise is usually opened by the most important person present, who leads off, draws in as many as he will, conducts them through stately manoeverings, winding up and down the dance space, with periodic bows, curtseys and flourishes. The activity of the leader is called *rej wodzic*, to lead, to have sway, an expression which has come into general use as a synonym—half mocking, half envious—for 'cock-of-the-walk'.

It has been said of the polonaise: 'It is the only (dance) of all which befits the man, which will not detract from the dignity of any age; for this reason it is the dance of monarchs, of heroes and even of old men. It expresses no passion, but seems to be a triumphal march, an expression of knightly feeling held in leash. And so it is characterized by solemn dignity. . . .'*

Pomerania, lying north of Great Poland, represents the only Polish outlet to the sea. Its coastal strip is one of several features that differentiate it from the rest of Poland. Before 1946 that strip—terminating the famous Polish corridor—was very limited. Since World War II there have been changes in territory and population that will radically change the picture.

Although the Baltic is an inland sea, its ports were always active in commerce and communication with other seas. The major Polish port—which is equivalent to saying the major Pomeranian port—has been Gdynia. It was acquired too recently to affect the basic culture picture of Pomerania. For the peasants the proximity of the sea has meant chiefly an opportunity for sea fishing, and for renting lodgings to seafarers. It has also brought tourist trade, since the sea is second only to the mountains as a Polish pleasure resort.

* An unforgettable picture of the polonaise is given by Mickiewicz in *Pan Tadeusz*, translated into English by George Rapall Noyes.

The coastal area consists chiefly of sand beaches, flat marshes and peat bogs. To the south of it lies a belt of lakes and pleasant wooded hills reaching to six or seven hundred feet.

The nucleus of the Pomeranian population is Cassoubian —a remnant of the Slavic Pomeranians who once occupied the entire tract between the lower Vistula and the Oder. In religion the Cassoubians are predominantly Protestant, so that this area is less overwhelmingly Catholic than most of Poland.

The Cassoubians are a provident people, for the most part small land-owners, industrious and frugal. Their cottages, of brick and timber gaily decorated with coloured washes, are well furnished and scrupulously clean. The level of education is relatively high—the illiteracy rate is one of the lowest in the country.

The soil of Pomerania is not especially productive. Although agriculture is the chief occupation of the region as a whole, fishing predominates on the coast and through the lake belt, and stock breeding is carried on in the uplands. About the northern areas the fisherman's joke says that people used to have only one cow and not enough food even for her. In order to keep her alive they made her green glasses. The cow, seeing the sand through the green glasses, thought it was grass and ate it, and that is how she remained alive.

Today real poverty is unknown in the fishing villages of the peninsula, as a result of the very interesting development of co-operative fishing societies to which most of the fishermen belong. Each society has its assigned fishing-ground, which is shifted each year, and no one else is allowed to fish in the allotted places. Fishing is done in common, and the proceeds are divided according in fixed proportions. The village priest and the teacher share in the catch, as do widows and the sick. A married fisherman receives a full share; a widow, half a share; an adult woman, a child, and a priest, a quarter share. The same rules apply to the sharing of hay.

In addition to the dances found throughout Poland, the fisherfolk of the maritime district have several of their own, some performed around the big dragnet during the carnival season. During this season they also dance the *wiwat*, a nimble performance executed while holding a mug of beer in one hand. Unlike most Polish dances, this one is performed only by men.

The folk costumes of Pomerania have almost disappeared. When they were still in evidence the most popular colour was dark blue, especially for the men's long coats with shoulder capes. The women's blouses, made with high necks and many tucks, were worn under gold-embroidered black bodices laced in front with a coloured ribbon; their skirts were red or white, their aprons white. On holidays large flowered shawls were worn, and bonnets embroidered in gold or silver. Those who live near the Baltic are fond of amber for necklaces, and the sea-colours of blue and green are prominent in their embroideries.

Silesia is the most densely populated region of Poland and the most highly industrialized, with an important mining area containing rich deposits of coal, iron, lead and zinc. The chief cities are Bytom and Katowice.

The cities and towns have a considerable German population with an additional scattering of Czechs. Despite the influence of both these groups, the working people in this region have clung steadfastly to their Polish culture. Their zeal may have been quickened by the endless friction between themselves and the German population, accentuated by a difference in religion—the Poles being Catholic and the Germans Protestant.

Nevertheless, Silesia is considered the most Germanized of

all the regions, both in its degree of industrialization and in the temper of its people.

The stubborn clinging to Polish culture in defiance of foreign influence dates back for centuries. Polish Slavs have inhabited Silesia since the fifth century. In the thirteenth century the country was devastated by the Tartars and the dukes attracted numerous German colonists who began to Germanize the land when the province was detached from Poland. The dukes and nobles soon became German and only the rural population remained Polish. It has preserved its character until the present time.

In the cities most people wear cosmopolitan dress, but in the countryside the traditional costume has survived. The men wear fur caps, blue jackets with shiny buttons and leather trousers. A curious feature of the women's costume is the cap of starched white lace and muslin—some resembling a garden hat with a squared crown and broad floppy brim.

The Carpathian mountains on the southern boundary of Poland, with the surrounding sub-Carpathian area, form the smallest of the six culture regions in size but perhaps the richest in colour and interest. It is the region least touched by modern industrial and urban influences. In recent years the tourist market and the enthusiasm of folk-minded individuals from the city have put new value on the preservation of old ways.

There are several mountainous regions in Poland and all are closer to each other in culture than to the neighbouring plainsfolk. The natives of the lofty Tatra area, however, are regarded as—and are—the very essence of the Polish mountaineer. They form also a separate entity in Polish folk life. Their history, their economy, their customs, their temperament, all show features at variance with the peasant norm.

In the eyes of the lowlanders, and very definitely in their own eyes, the mountaineers—*Gorale*—stand apart from other Polish peasants. They represent glamour, romance and daring: combining the elements of Robin Hood, the American cowboy, and a touch of Francois Villon. They also represent to some of their carping neighbours, improvidence, restlessness and laziness.

The very name *Gorale* has come to mean pride, dash, and courage, the triumph of honour. In this respect they represent independence, the prime ingredient in being Polish according to the Poles. They boast that their ancestors were never serfs and feel that this history of freedom from servitude, plus their other virtues and distinctions, makes them superior to those of their fellow countrymen whose ancestors submitted to the indignities of feudalism.

The mountaineers were stateless for centuries, living in complete independence and having little contact with the valleys and cities. The forbidding terrain, so much more difficult to invaders than to its native defenders, helped the *Gorale* to ward off domination and tyranny. The proud spirit with which they resisted oppression gained new pride through the success of that resistance.

The heights inhabited by the *Gorale* rise some three thousand feet above the rest of the range. For the most part the Carpathian mountains are pleasant grassy or wooded slopes averaging about five thousand feet. On the Polish-Czech border, however, they culminate in the Tatra group, close to eight thousand feet in elevation, and of truly Alpine splendour. The granite peaks and ridges are lofty, steep and dangerous, their jagged heights bare to the wind or glittering with snow and ice. Forests of fir and spruce extending up the mountain slopes are the home of animals extinct elsewhere in Poland. At about forty-eight hundred feet the forests give way to rich pasture land where the mountaineers raise livestock. Their homes, just below the pastures, are far above their nearest neighbours.

From the age of five or six the *Gorale* is accustomed to roaming the dangerous and jagged peaks, making the split-second decision that mountain-climbing demands. Even when they stride along on level ground they show the bold grace, fine co-ordination, and zestful assurance won on the heights.

A favourite sport among the young men is to pluck for their sweethearts the Alpine flower *szarotka* that grows only under a cliff on the north side of the mountain, always in a spot dangerous to reach. Unlike most flowers, it can be dried and kept. A girl is proud to wear the Alpine flower in her hair, and it is a great favourite in the Tatra as an ornament or as the theme for a decorative design.

The economy of the *Gorale* is pastoral and not agricultural. Their chief income is from cattle, which they raise in large numbers on the rich pasture-lands lying just above their high homes. The secondary source is sheep, which are grazed still higher up in the mountains. In addition, they are excellent hunters and magnificent woodcutters and lumbermen, who know how to exploit cleverly the forests covering the mountain slopes to supply logs to the valley below.

The few crops they cultivate are oats, barley and potatoes, but the bread they eat comes from the farms down in the valleys. Because they are non-agricultural, the *Gorale* do not venerate and value land as do the people of the plains. Nor do they have the system of inheritance and farmer 'abdication' that so strongly tinges the whole social life of the lowlanders, with the tensions and conflicts that have grown up about that system.

They are more relaxed and free in other respects also—in their attitudes toward sex, in their dealings with strangers, and in their general behaviour. They seem to be gayer and to enjoy life more.

They blame nature for their lack of agricultural diligence —the soil is poor. But their neighbours point out that the soil is poor in most of present-day Poland and nobody refrains from tilling it on that account. They feel that the mountaineers are lazy and unstable, turning from one thing to another, not wanting to settle and be tied down to farm life. So, though they admire and enjoy the verve of the *Gorale,* they also criticize their shiftless ways. Thus, each group retains a comforting sense of superiority.

The agriculturalists in the sub-Carpathian region have much in common with other Polish peasants, besides their agriculture and their attitudes toward the *Gorale.* Their land, unlike much that is now being cultivated in Poland, is known for its fertility. The supply is so limited, however, that even the richest peasants have no more than twenty *morgs,* or about twenty-eight acres. The small harvests they normally expect are sometimes lost because of the winds that rage down from the mountains, or because the spring is late and the snow stays on the ground far into the planting season.

As snow melts on the grazing grounds, or *hale,* there is a great exodus of sheep flocks to their pastures. This is quite a ceremonial occasion, called *kierdale.* In the autumn a similar migration takes place in the opposite direction.

A *hala* is a grazing ground owned jointly by a group of villages having shares which entitle them to keep so many 'tails' of sheep or cattle on each. The shares, therefore, are called 'tails'. Normally there is no marked boundary between the *hale,* which form geographical entities divided from each other by mountains or forests.

Mountaineers who own sheep in addition to their cattle usually hire a special shepherd to guard the flocks. This senior shepherd, called the *baca,* in turn employs junior shepherds to tend the flocks under his direction. The *baca* is absolute master of the flocks and the owner has no voice in their management.

There is an elaborate code regulating the relationship of the junior and senior shepherds, and the duties of each. There is also a definite series of steps by which a junior shepherd advances to the rank of senior, beginning with menial tasks such as cooking for the other shepherds and working upward.

While they are up in the *hale,* the men live in special shelters consisting of one large room. In many shelters the sleeping berths are high shelves, below the roof. The shelters have no chimneys so that the smoke escapes through the roof, smoking the cheeses that are festooned along the side beams of the roof racks.

The shepherds' food is very frugal and consists of a sort of buttermilk left from the sheep's milk after it has been made into cheese, oat cake, potatoes. Meat is a very rare addition to this diet.

White sheep dogs which resemble St. Bernards are kept on chains and are often quite dangerous, particularly if their master's possessions are tampered with.

The mountaineers are far more mobile than their fellow-countrymen of the lowland. In summer they often migrate to other countries—Czechoslovakia, Germany, Hungary—to do seasonal work. They tend not to specialize in a single trade but like to do every kind of task. For example, it is not unusual for one man to combine the skills of smith, carpenter, plumber, wagon-driver, mountain-guide and maker of bronze ornaments. They also make most of their own clothes, except for the sheepskin jackets which they wear, and their hats which they buy in the city.

They even make their own shoes, which are mocassin style and very comfortable for walking—constructed from one piece of leather stitched together across the top and gathered around the edges with a thong. Many of these shoes are sold to tourists, who contribute an important part to the local economy. The Poles love mountain climbing and they flock to the Tatra in large numbers, swelling the income and also the ego of the *Gorale*.

In appearance as well as in temperament the mountaineers are the most romantic of all the Poles. They appreciate their own picturesque glamour and are always ready to pose for camera-clicking tourists. The typical *Goral* is tall, erect, slim, usually with dark straight hair and a contented air of superiority. The women are endowed with dark and striking beauty, but they age very quickly.

Nowhere in Poland is there more love of finery and more joy in its display than among the highlanders of the Tatra. They are the only peasants who wear the traditional costume in all its glory every day and do not reserve it for Sundays and holidays. They wear much white which forms an effective background for bursts of flashing colour and gleaming ornaments.

The traditional costume of the men includes tight white wool trousers decorated with wide striped seams and embroidered in front with an ornament in bright red and blue called *parzenica*, which is characteristic of the *Gorale* and has a distinctive style for each group. It should be remarked that although they all refer to themselves as *Gorale*, the mountaineers are very conscious of the distinctions between the local groups inhabiting different peaks of the range.

The trousers are bound around the ankle when worn with the usual moccasins. For very special occasions, however, they are tucked into fine white felt boots which the mountaineers make both for themselves and for sale to tourists. The men's white blouses are heavy with embroidery, and they wear a very broad leather belt sometimes ten or twelve inches a cross and studded with brass studs.

Their small round hats are made of black felt, the low crowns encircled by a string of white mussel shells and with an eagle or falcon feather cocked to one side. Over the blouse an embroidered, sleeveless, fur-lined coat or *serdak* is often worn with a cape of short, loose, white cloth again frequently heavily embroidered. This garment is fastened in front with a broad red ribbon. When it rains the *serdak* is promptly reversed and worn with the fur outside in order to protect the embroidery.

An indispensable part of the costume is the large brass brooch, hung with trinkets and worn on the chest. Equally ornamental is the small, long-handled axe which is the inseparable companion of the *Goral*, serving as a dandy's swagger stick, a climber's aid, or a fighter's mace. Its head, usually of brass with a design incised in the blade, is particularly well adapted to hacking a foothold in the mountain ice. The wooden staff is sometimes covered with tin or brass.

These strong staves, topped by a metal blade, appear to be a survival of the ancient battle-axe. Elaborately ornamented with brass, they are in keeping with the armour-like belt and jingling metal brooch that suggests a miniature breast plate.

The women, less magnificent and also less glamorous than the men, are less preoccupied with their costumes and with self-admiration. It is noticeable, for example, that in dancing the man concentrates more on his own performance than on his partner, whereas in other regions he at least vouchsafes her a glance now and then.

Nevertheless the costumes of the women are far from drab. They wear full, figured skirts and tight dark velvet bodices embroidered with spangles and corals, laced down the front over white 'shirts' with embroidered sleeves. A favourite ornament is the necklace of multi-coloured beads in many strands. Their characteristic footgear is either the soft pointed moccasins, *kierpce*, made from one piece of leather, or high dark boots laced over white stockings. There are none of the elaborate headdresses familiar in other parts of Poland. The chief head covering is a coloured or flowered kerchief which the married women usually wear and the unmarried girls wear only as protection against sun or wind.

The homes and furniture of the mountaineers also bear the stamp of their outlandishness. Wood is plentiful in the Tatra, and the *Gorale* are master wood-workers, an art developed and practised through long hours of herding and pasturing. Their houses, their furniture, their utensils are carved with intricate and imaginative designs, often ambitiously fretted. The mountaineer wields his knife with the amazing facility that the lowlander shows with his scissors; wood-carving is as flexible, adroit, sprightly and abundant in the mountain regions as the art of paper cut-outs is in the farmlands.

The mountain homes often appear larger and more prosperous than those in most parts of Poland. Unlike the characteristic plain-land cottages, they are never whitewashed or tinted, but are left unpainted inside and out. Usually they have stone foundations beneath the heavy logs that form the upper part. The wooden beams are decorated with carving, and wooden ornaments top the front of the shingled roof. The shape of the door is also distinctive, curved at the top and surrounded with decoration.

When colour is used it is vivid, with many reds and greens, and here the red is less fuchsia and more red than in most regions. The most colourful ceramics of Poland are found in the mountains, where pottery is highly developed. All the arts and crafts find exuberant expression in the Tatra. It is from this area that city artists have drawn most heavily in cultivating the vogue of peasant art, just as Polish ethnographers have found most colour and interest in the lore and folkways of the *Gorale*.

The great stove of the mountain home is not whitewashed as in the rest of Poland, but is made of glazed bricks, each decorated with its own design. These bricks are among the few sorts of secular decoration in which the human figure is portrayed. Most of the folk art employs either floral or geometric patterns, and representation of the human figure is largely limited to religious uses. But the glazed bricks of the mountain stoves are often animated by pictures of human beings or of animals.

The most characteristic mountain dances are brigands' dances, quick, fiery, and requiring tremendous muscular agility. The dancer holds the long-handled axe that is almost a part of him, whirling it into the air as he dances and catching it again with a flourish. These dances are for men only, with the women participating as appreciative audience. The group brigands' dance has a great deal of leaping and crouching, swift movement in a circle, and the clashing of axe against axe. When the brigand's dance is performed as a solo, the ideal achievement is to leap so high into the air that the performer can cross his legs and fire a pistol before he touches ground again. Stamping and swaying, he sings:

> *Hey, I am making for the forest*
> *My feather waves and shines*
> *I am making for the forest*
> *And the earth rings as I stride!*

Almost from the time they can walk, boys begin training for expert dance performance, and ability to dance is among the prime social assets. Almost every Saturday night, and on any holiday, there will be a gathering where the chief entertainment is dancing. The privilege of commanding the dance will be captured by some enterprising man who, after consuming enough vodka to inspire him, will instruct the orchestra to play the melody he wants. To be really clever he must improvise words to the traditional tune and make them as funny and topical as he can. It is a point of pride for him to supply his own words, which he sings before he begins dancing. He pays the orchestra for each melody they play for him.

The chief performer selects a girl to be his partner, and two of her girl friends will dance with her for a little before she joins the man. From then on no one will stop him unless he stops himself. If some other man wants to dance before the first one stops, he must ask permission to 'dance for' the original performer, and will then dance with the same girl. If a man refuses to give others a chance, there may be fights for the floor. In order to prevent violence, the women usually try to persuade the dancer to share his spotlight.

Mountain folklore is the ethnographer's delight, as mountain art is the joy of the urban artist. It has retained its vitality and variety through centuries of untrammelled development, and has remained a functioning part of daily life. Schools and even churches became common relatively late in the mountains. The body of folklore remained a vital part of the individual's education, and long hours of watching in the pasture or of biding one's time during bad weather in the home gave abundant opportunity for the exchange of tales and songs.

There are many stories about Tartar invasion and many tales of local heroes. The ideal hero of the mountain area is of the Robin Hood type, the best known being Janosik. Epic songs are popular among the Carpathians, and are often sung by wandering bards to groups of people gathered in the market place.

Several dances have been mentioned with the regions of which they are especially characteristic. Each region has its

THE PARTS OF THE WHOLE

own type and manner of dancing, influenced by external contacts as well as by native patterns. Yet the role of the dance has been so special and most of the dances—with whatever local variation—are so widely diffused through Poland, that a word about folk dances in general must be added.

Not only does each region and often each locality have its own dance style and preference. Each outstanding performer dances *po swojemu,* in his own way. All group dances, however, are directed by a leader—the *przodkujacy* or *stojacy na takcie*—who, with his partner, forms the first couple.

Since the onlookers sing the words to the dances, stamp out the rhythm and sometimes sway to it, the whole group participates to some extent. For all its inclusiveness, however, the folk dancing would not be Polish if it were not also individualistic and competitive. Sometimes tournaments are arranged, and people from nearby villages come to compete —far less often today than in the past, to be sure. The losers feel no social compulsion to be good sports about their defeat. If the 'foreigners' from another village get the better of them, they will find ways to get even. At a wedding, if a guest from another village out-dances the local blades, they feel affronted and may manage to pick a fight with him before the end.

In some dances the song goes on without interruption, in others a soloist sings first and the chorus answers him; in still others there is singing with part of the dance and only instrumental music for the rest. The melodies frequently fall into two parts—the first lyrical and slow, the second gay, quick in tempo, an outburst of energy.

The dance orchestra varies according to region, location, economic resources, and the importance of the occasion. A full dance orchestra would include several violins, cello, flute, clarinet, horn, bass viol, and a *gensla* which is a sort of zither. In the mountains an instrument like a flute, but several feet long, is used. A full orchestra, however, is not at all necessary to full enjoyment—fortunately, since it is very seldom met with. But a fiddle alone, or a harmonica, or merely the voices of the spectators and the rhythmic stamping of feet can call the tune.

In former times dancing was much more common than during the last few decades. But the Poles still love it and strike up on every possible occasion. They wear their finest clothes at a dance party, relishing the opportunity to indulge in the equally enjoyed exercise of dressing up.

Most of the social dances are performed by men and women in pairs. Only in the mountain regions are solo dances by men the most popular. In other sections a few special dances are for men or for women only, but often these dances are at least semi-ritualistic in character. The *wiwat* danced by the Pomeranian fishermen is an example; among dances for women only are the celebration of the *korowaj* or wedding cake by the women who bake it, and the dance at the Tavern on Shrove Tuesday.

It has been pointed out, however, that even when couples dance, the man is apt to be the chief performer, with the woman acting as his foil. In the majority of Polish dances, the performers are arranged in rows of couples, threes or fours, standing so that the girls are always on the outside of the line and the boys on the side towards the centre.

Two basic dances are distributed under different names and with many variations throughout Poland; the mazurka, described in the opening chapter, is the principal dance in uneven time; the *krakowiak* the principal one in even time.

Three variants of the mazurka or *mazur* are familiar: the *mazurek*, the *kujawiak*, and the *oberek* or *obertas*. The three differ in tempo and in rhythm. The *mazur* and the *oberek* are square dances with a great variety of figures. Their tunes are swift and gay and the steps are intricate, requiring great skill. In the *oberek*, for instance, the man has to drop alternately to his right and left knee while whirling his partner around. The girl, too, must be surefooted in order not to lose her balance or fall out of step while her partner keeps hopping up and down by her side.

The *kujawiak* is slower than either the *mazurek* or the *oberek*, less 'jumpy', more 'polished', more sedate. It is danced round and round, without emphasis or stamping. Moreover, unlike the others, it has no definite end but goes on and on in a never-ending circle.

The true *kujawiak* can be seen only in the Kujawy neighbourhood of northeast Mazovia, although something very close to it is danced in western Poland. Many of the so-called *kujawiaki* are either *oberki* or *mazurki*. The people of Kujaway begin the dance with the *spiacy* or 'sleeping *kujawiak*'. The dancers place their hands on the upper forearms of their partners and turn in a circle to the left, slowly and dreamily at first, then gradually quickening their pace and turning now left, now right.

The *krakowiak* is next to the polonaise in point of age. Formerly it was danced only by the nobility except in its native Krakow where all people dance it. Today it has been adopted by the folk throughout the country. The music of the *krakowiak* is gay and lively.

The *golabek*, a dance for four, is known in certain sections of Silesia where a number of old dances have persisted, including the *lipka* and the *trojok* or dance for three.

Two very old dances which have survived in only a few places are the *szewc* and the *owczarz*. The latter is named for the shepherd, *owczarz*, who leads the eight couples performing the dance, and carries a big cudgel. As they perform a series of steps, the dancers sing a song beginning:

K

A ragamuffin is tending cattle and a ragged girl, sheep
The ragamuffin wants the ragged girl
But she does not want him.

When the stanza is ended, the *owczarz* pounds on the floor with his cudgel, whereupon the girls and youths separate and draw up in two rows facing each other. The *owczarz* stands in the middle and the young men begin bargaining for the 'sheep'—that is, the girls. When the facetious and often boisterous bargaining is concluded, the *owczarz* throws his cudgel to the ground and seizes one of the 'sheep'. The young men hastily try to snatch a partner and whoever fails to get one becomes the new *owczarz*. Then the dance and song begin again.

The ritual dances included in the holiday festivals and other special celebrations are more uniform than the purely social dances throughout the country. Words, music and steps show far less local variation since value is put on adhering strictly to tradition in dances of this type. Nevertheless, for the most part the ritual significance of the dances performed on St. John's Eve, Shrove Tuesday, and other holidays has dropped into the background, and they too are regarded primarily as a source of pleasure.

V THE HOME CIRCLE

Molto allegro, con vigore.

THE FAMILY IS the all important unit in peasant life—an economic, a social and a religious unit. A son or an unmarried daughter who leaves home still remains part of that unit. A holy wafer will be sent to each absent member at Christmas time, as symbol of his continuing place in the family circle. A girl who goes into domestic service in the city may send money home to help in the upkeep of her brothers and sisters. Once a year she will probably return for a week to help harvest the potatoes. A boy who goes to the city to work or to seek an education, will often return to marry, receive his share of the family farm, and settle down in his native village.

The importance of the family unit has been evident in the holiday festivities. The elaborate preparations, the feasts, the holiday attire, are primarily for home consumption, rather than for the pleasure and participation of outsiders.

There may be, and very often are, strong tensions within the family group. Fathers are strict and stern with their children, especially their sons. Sons are often hostile toward each other and fiercely rebellious against the parental authority. The inheritance system in itself builds up resentments and antagonisms. Yet these internal conflicts create no visible breach in the solid front presented by the family unit. All will band together against any outsider, all will rally to the defence of any member who is attacked or threatened from beyond the close-knit circle of blood relationship.

The bond is not necessarily one of affection. There is remarkably little expression of affection between members of the family and they seldom speak of each other in terms of warm feeling. There appears to be as much concern for economic status and stability, and for 'face', as for emotional bonds. The family is an economic unit and it is also a social corporation, reinforced by the strongest traditional sanctions. All the village may know that two brothers are in constant conflict. But all the village would be shocked if those same brothers failed to stand together against any onslaught—even a justified one—from beyond the kinship circle. The saying *krew nie woda,* 'blood is not water', has great force and wide currency. If a family is against one of its members, or a man is publicly at odds with his family, it is taken as a sign that somehow he is not what he should be.

The Polish peasant family unit is striking for its extent as well as for its stability and authority. The term *swojak,* kinsman, is applied to all relatives and in-laws to the third degree of kinship—that is, including second cousins.

To be called *swojak* implies both responsibilities and privileges. Mutual help of all kinds—legal, financial, moral— is appropriate to all members of the group covered. Among other claims is the right of residence when a family member is temporarily in need of a home, and sometimes even when he is permanently without one. It may not follow that the claim will be met gladly or graciously, but it is recognized.

The father's side of the family is called the 'sword side' and the mother's the 'distaff side' in Poland as in many other countries. That both sides are of equal importance is a commentary on the structure of the Polish family.

MARRIAGE

The family begins with marriage. In a sense the individual adult also begins with marriage, for a Polish peasant who fails to marry fails to achieve complete human stature. As one peasant put it, 'a man becomes really a man when he marries.'

Marriage is regarded as a 'holy duty' and celibacy as a state contrary to nature. A bachelor or spinster past marriageable age is an object of censure, scorn and ridicule. They are addressed by the familiar 'thou' employed for children and social inferiors, rather than by 'you' as befits a dignified adult.

The mockery and penalties visited on the unmarried during the pre-Lenten holidays are far from serious but are also nevertheless unpleasant. More sustained and more burdensome are the year-round, day by day penalties of unmarried sisters or brothers who live 'on the kindness of the family'. Their status is inferior, or rather it might be said that they have no status. There is no social or economic role for them in the family or in the village. No matter how cordial the family relations, they remain outside the inner circle and have to take pains to win the good graces of brother or sister, nephews and nieces.

No one would dare ask an old bachelor why he had not married and he himself would not dream of offering an explanation, because bachelorhood is considered a calamity and the suspicion is always that something must be wrong with the man. Still worse is an old maid's lot. A girl is destined for marriage from the hour of her birth and therefore is regarded as only a temporary member of the immediate family. She is considered an economic liability rather than an asset to her parents, and they look forward to the day when a suitor will take her off their hands.

While she is still young and attractive she too looks forward to that day. Her mother sees that she is dressed becomingly and her father looks after her support. Every effort is made to provide her with a dowry and to secure a likely suitor.

If she fails to marry in the normal time, however, she has to suffer not only her own disappointment but also the disappointment, scorn and resentment of her family, and the disdain of the whole community. She is a poor creature indeed. Young men shun her at dances where 'she sells onions', as the saying describes the perennial wallflower. Even after death the fate pursues her, for in the hereafter 'she will pasture stallions and goats'.

Fortunately, very few Polish peasants of either sex need remain unmarried. Only uncommonly ill-favoured girls, or girls with a bad reputation remain single—especially if they lack a dowry. Parents will go to great lengths to find a suitable spouse, if the issue appears in doubt. If at last a girl gives up hope of marrying at home, she may go to the city. Here her possibilities will be increased, not only by numbers but also because if necessary she can marry beneath her station. To marry 'beneath herself' would be far more difficult in the village where at all costs the family must maintain face. Status is what really matters, and to have a child marry beneath the status of the family would lower the standing of the parents and the whole household.

So strong is the feeling against misalliance that parents have been known to forbid marriage between their daughter and the father of her illegitimate child, if the man's status made him an unsuitable fiance—preferring to adopt the child themselves. Such an attitude is rare, however. Most parents would consider their daughter's fall an indelible stain on the family honour and would be eager to erase it out by having her marry the man.

Aside from special exigencies, it is assumed that marriage should be contracted between people of equal status—and the chief criterion of status is land ownership. A village cobbler or blacksmith should not aspire to the hand of a landed peasant's daughter, for even the poorest landowner has more status than any landless artisan. That a farmhand who works on another's fields should marry a landowner's daughter is next to unthinkable and would be viewed as a desperate last resort. Yet in other respects, farmhands are socially accepted, treated like members of the household and included with the family at meals. The tendency to match economic status is fostered by the dowry arrangements, since a very poor father could hardly meet the settlement demaned by a prosperous one.

The marriage partner is usually selected from within the village. Young men are advised not to marry an outsider. 'If the girl is good, a local man will take her before you—a stranger will get only what nobody in the village wants.' If a man does take a wife from outside, he offends the local community, especially the women. 'Haven't we right fine girls here in the village?' they will ask. And they treat the newcomer unkindly until she manages to gain their good graces. One result of this in-breeding is the development of strong physical similarity between the members of localities where the custom remains in force.

There is, however, a widely observed prohibition against marriage among blood relatives. For the most part, very distant kinship is not a barrier but in some regions even third cousins are considered too closely related for marriage. Although the church gives its dispensation to second cousins, people will cite examples to prove that such marriages do not succeed. Marriage between godparent and godchild is frowned upon, since the relationship is regarded as real. Though such marriages have occurred with increasing frequency in recent years, the belief persists that children of such unions do not thrive and the spouses themselves are often sickly.

The marriages of the brothers and sisters in a family are usually timed according to seniority. The oldest marries first and the others follow in the order of their ages. Where the father is dead, an only brother will often postpone his own marriage until all his sisters have found husbands.

In the old days it was taken for granted that parents or guardians would arrange for the unions of young people. Only a bachelor of many years standing would decide and act for himself, although forced marriages very seldom occur. In recent years there has been an increasing tendency to consider the wishes of the young people, but it is still generally assumed that the final decision does not rest with them.

Although postponing marriage too long is an invitation to public censure, as well as to scorn and ridicule, it is not customary for Polish peasants to marry very young. As a rule the men do not marry before they are twenty-three and many of them wait until their thirties, working at home, serving a term as hired help, and of course completing their required military service. Girls are most likely to marry between seventeen and twenty. For some it may be later, for the saying is that they must first work for their parents to earn a dowry.

The parents of a marriageable girl often announce their readiness to bestow her hand by means of certain well-known signs that vary from region to region: daubing the cottage with dots of paint, placing potted flowers on the window sill, or hanging a wreath on the door. Other decorations about the cottage may less officially announce the presence of a marriageable girl.

Most of the holiday decorations are made by girls, because once a woman is married she has little time for such frivolity. Even though the girls help a great deal in their parents' homes, the home is not their primary responsibility. Only at harvest time are they too busy to exercise their skill in arts and decoration. Once they are married, their own home will be their own responsibility and it will probably leave them neither time nor energy for the maidenly, as compared with the housewifely arts.

Girls enjoy decorating their homes, not only because they take pride in their skill but also because tasteful and ingenious decorations help to advertise their feminine virtues. Ability to make delighful paper cut-outs will not be required of the housewife, but such ability suggests proficiency in the womanly tasks of a good home-maker.

For the most part there is no need to call attention to the eligibility of a man. If a man is deformed or crippled, however, it may be considered necessary to announce that he is in the marriage market. This is done by betrothing him to a cousin or some other relative and having the banns read in church—with no idea that a marriage will follow, but merely to publish his marriage ability. This device is known as *wystawic sie*, to display oneself standing up, that is to show that one is qualified to stand up with the rest. The expected sequel is that he will then be considered seriously.

Lucky is the pair who fall in love and have the approval of their parents, for if there is conflict, the parents' will—based on economic and social considerations—is likely to prevail over romantic love. Yet, as in most places where marriages are arranged, romantic love does assert itself and often it is possible to reconcile inclination and expediency. The foremost requirement in a mate may be the possession of land. Nevertheless, if one were not wholly landless, personal qualifications are bound to make themselves felt. Regardless of one's dowry, it is well to be beautiful, charming, gifted; to dance with fire and grace; to be expert with needle and scissors as well as with scythe and hoe.

Since marriage mates are usually chosen from within the village, they have probably known each other as small

children; yet often their meeting in youth is like a redis-
covery. The young man is usually older and has been away in
the army or perhaps in the city, while the girl was growing
from childhood into girlhood. Accordingly there is no lack of
the surprise and discovery element, or of strong romantic
attachment such as is found in many parts of the world. But
the village is small, and the choice is limited by requirements
as well as by numbers.

Marriage, obviously, is not a simple affair between two
individuals, but a complicated transaction involving their
families and the community. Not only does the opinion of
family and community dictate the choice of the partner, but
they have a very active part in the arrangement and celebration of the rites—the role of the bridal pair being largely
passive throughout.

In addition to its religious and social significance, the
marriage ritual expresses, as one ethnologist has said, 'the
sanction given by an agrarian community to a pair of
agriculturists embarking upon the earning of their own
agrarian bread'. As in all the peasant ceremonials, Christian
and pre-Christian elements mingle closely, and every
observance carries overtones that may condition and foretell
the future. In fact the importance attributed to omens and
auspices throughout the wedding ceremonies has been so
great that as early as 1279 the church forbade the practice of
divination at weddings, under pain of excommunication.

As befits a step important not only to the individuals but
also to the group, the marriage ceremonies are never hasty or
impromptu, but are carried out in a series of formalized
procedures extending over several months—the wedding itself usually lasts for several days. The protracted ritual
accounts for the saying, 'On Our Lady of the Candles, adieu
my handsome one', for if he has not proposed by February 2,
there will not be time to conclude the formalities before Lent.

The ceremonies themselves have the structure of a play divided into episodes or acts, which by their function have an essential unity. These acts are not identical in all localities, do not always occur at the same time intervals, and may show minor variations in order. Yet despite infinite variety in detail, the basic pattern is constant. The acts are: 1 *wywiady*— inquiry and proposal; 2 *zareczyny* or *zrekowiny*—betrothal; 3 *dziewiczy wieczor*—maiden evening (unbraiding); 4 *korowaj* —baking the wedding cake; 5 *wesele*—marriage ceremony 6 *pokladziny*—putting to bed; 7 *oczepiny*—capping; 8 *przenosiny*—removal to the groom's home.

The wedding drama has a number of fixed roles. It has a chorus, whose members are the separate retinues of the bride and groom. It has dances, both ritual and social; it has certain fixed properties and decorations. It may even be said to have a book, in the manual of orations, toasts and songs used by the various functionaries—although in fact they depend more on tradition and experience than on the printed pages, some dating back to the sixteenth century, which few peasants can read. Perhaps the chief respect in which this drama differs from a theatrical play is that although it is an elaborately staged spectacle it is at the same time a part of real life, and a crucial part.

The principals are not unaware of the dramatic nature of the marriage rites. In selecting their cast of characters they try to choose those who not only will do them honour by their status in the community but will also insure a smooth, impressive, and auspicious performance. The roles of parents and other near relatives are of course filled automatically. The selection of 'choruses'—bridesmaids, ushers, guests—is also determined largely by blood relationship and friendship. But for the key action roles—matchmakers, master of ceremonies, best man, maid of honour, matron of honour— persons are chosen who possess native gifts of eloquence, wit, geniality, good memory, in addition to practised familiarity with the local tradition. In short, the key performing members of the cast should have a talent for histrionics.

Among the most important of these functionaries is the matchmaker, or *swat*, who first conveys the marriage proposal. He may or may not serve later as master of ceremonies at the wedding, where his wife may be the matron of honour. The matchmaker, or 'proposer', is sometimes called *raj* or *dziewoslab*. If, as very rarely happens, a woman serves as matchmaker, she is called *swatka, staroscina,* or *gadulina.* In some localities the roles of master of ceremonies and matron of honour pass from father to son and from mother to daughter, but though their skill is almost professional, their office is purely honorific and performed without pay.

Throughout the wedding ceremonies, and especially on the wedding day, most of the singing is done in chorus—often in two choruses. The bride's retinue addresses or challenges the groom's retinue; the bridesmaids, headed by the maid of honour, sing in opposition to the married women, who, led by the matron of honour, then respond. There is singing also by the guests at the table, praising the food and thanking their hosts.

In general the singing supplements, describes, or give the cue for action, and is essentially ritual in character. But there is also singing for amusement only, and such 'incidental music' may be drawn from any source—soldiers' songs, songs from the theatre, popular ballads. There is improvisation too, and solo-singing at least of a verse, until the crowd catches on or joins in the chorus. This happens especially during the dancing.

Unlike the singing, which is chiefly ritual in character, the dancing is done primarily for amusement, expressing the general gaiety and joy. Even the few wedding dances that are ritual in origin have lost any solemn significance they may have had. (It is a tradition that each man must dance with the bride and with every woman and girl at the wedding itself. To say that one has danced at a person's wedding implies a claim of close friendship.)

When the parents agree that 'the boy's time has come', or when the young man has made his choice and obtained their consent, they take steps to find out whether his suit will be welcomed. This process is known as *wywiady*—inquiry or sounding out; or as *udawanie sie w komplementa*, paying compliments. More colloquially it is often called *poslac z wodka*, going with vodka, bringing vodka; or *poslac swatow*, sending the proposers.

One or two friends of the family are asked to call on the girl's parents as matchmakers. They are usually substantial married people who enjoy high status in the community, as well as outstanding powers of persuasion, tact and social ability. Their mission is a delicate one for *wywiady* is dedicated to the all-important pattern of face-saving. Its function is not merely to find out if the suit is acceptable, but to do so in a way that will 'protect' the 'honour' of the suitor and of his family. This, it is felt, can be accomplished only through indirect suggestion.

There is no mistaking the purpose of the delegation as it approaches the girl's home. The matchmakers, dressed in their very best, wear over one shoulder the long, richly embroidered ceremonial towel—a mark of office and also a sign that the occasion is a joyous one. In some localities, they may wear a special feather in their hats or a flower *boutonniere* on their coats, as a badge of their mission. Moreover, in his hand or conspicuously bulging out of his pocket, the chief matchmaker carries the vodka that he hopes will seal the agreement.

On entering the cottage, the matrimonial ambassadors greet their hosts with the usual 'Praise the Lord!' and then hint at their purpose in veiled terms designed to fool nobody.

They say they are travellers from afar, seeking shelter for the night—could they find it here? Or that they want to buy a heifer, do the hosts perhaps have one for sale? Or that they have lost a goose, could it have strayed to this place?

If their hosts—who seldom would be taken by surprise at this visitation—have decided to reject the suit without further discussion, they would answer with courtesy and regret. No, unfortunately they have no rooms to spare: or no, alas, the heifer is not for sale; or no lost goose has wandered in here. The device is immaterial, the 'no' all-important. And everyone can pretend that nothing was said about marriage, thus preserving the dignity of the ambassadors, the suitor, and his family. It is seldom that parents reject a suitor in this earliest stage, however, because 'every girl wants it to be known that she is in demand', and such 'compliments' may stir up competition.

If the suitor is not to be rejected, the answer to the matchmakers will be, 'Why yes, we think we have just what you are looking for.' Thus encouraged, the visitors set their vodka on the table and the young man is called in.

At this point the parents sometimes tell him what the dowry will be, and that he should consider well whether its small size may not weaken his attachment as time goes on. If he vows that it will not, and if they have no further misgivings, they give their consent and the girl is summoned.

Usually she is close at hand. Decency requires that she be out of the room during the preliminary negotiations, but she is apt to remain near enough to appear promptly when called. She must act reluctant and frightened when she enters, as if she wanted to run away. The suitor may join in the game, barring the door and pursuing her as she cries out for help and runs to shelter in the alcove or near the stove. The bridesmaids will sing about this on the wedding day:

When the matchmaker comes
I'll be sitting by the stove
I shall pretend to be sad
But in truth I'll be glad.

If the girl at last allows herself to be caught and accepts a drink from the hand of the suitor or a go-between, it is a sign that she consents. She will turn her face to the wall, as any well brought up girl should do in drinking, to show her modesty and good manners. If she is very shy or very genteel, she may throw her apron over her head as she drinks.

After the formalities, all join in drinking vodka together, both for good cheer and as a symbol of a binding agreement. Even in concluding the sale of cattle at the fairs, vodka serves as a sign and seal.

Both marriage partners receive a dowry. If the suitor's parents participate in the proposal visit, the dowry arrangements may be settled at once. If not, a separate visit may be made later to arrange details, although the match would hardly be agreed upon without a general understanding about the marriage settlement. In either case, the young people have no part in the dowry negotiations, which are the concern of their parents and the matchmakers.

The dowry represents the family's importance and status, as well as the economic endowment of the young couple. As a rule it is given by the parents, although grandparents, brother, uncle, or godparents may give all or part of it. Usually the groom's family provides the land, or most of it, because land counts for more than money and the husband who settles on his wife's land loses standing. If the bride is an heiress and an only child, the husband might bring only money. In this case he would occupy an inferior status, since his wife would be the landowner. She would have the better of him in quarrels, and would have little respect for his opinions.

When the girl does receive land, either as part of her dowry or by inheritance, it remains hers for life. Her husband merely manages it and when she dies it is inherited by her children. This is called *babizna*, or mother's land, as opposed to *ojcowizna* or father's land.

Inquiries about the girl's dowry must be made with discretion. The matchmaker may ask, 'How much did your daughter earn during her service?' The father usually has sole discretion in determining what dowry his daughter shall have. If she receives the amount in full, she must sign a release stating that she will make no further claims on her father's property. On behalf of the groom, his father has a legal document drawn up, stating what his son will receive from him, and the dowry he is to get from the bride's father.

In old times there were no written agreements. The transaction was made 'on good word' or 'on faith' with no seal more legal than the binding draught of vodka. Often the father promised much more than he could pay, and then there would be quarrels and lawsuits. Later the agreement came to be signed in the presence of a public notary, so that payment is assured to the future husband and the girl has a written record of what should remain her own.

The girl's dowry consists chiefly of money, clothing, household goods, perhaps a heifer. The clothing, bedding and linens have been gathered through the years, ever since her early childhood, and stored in a hope chest which the Poles call *skrzynia*—among the most colourful and important pieces of household furniture. The chests are usually painted in gay colours with a double flower and leaf design, symbolizing the marriage union of two individuals. The dowry heifer or cow may be one that was given to her as a newborn calf and brought up by her with tender care, as her very own —a barnyard extension to the hope chest.

MARRIED WOMAN'S COSTUME FROM OPOCZNO, LODZ DISTRICT

TOWN COSTUMES FROM THE ZYWIEC REGION

Even if a large money settlement is made on the bride, it is seldom enough to buy a farm, enabling her to preserve the status she enjoyed before marriage. In any case, her family would seldom allow her to marry a poor man, for that would be taken as proof that she was without ambition and therefore must have some personal defect. There are of course a few exceptions to the rule of economic equality in marriage arrangements. For example, if a young man receives a very large portion of land from his father, a healthy and industrious girl, rather than a wealthy one, may be sought.

The bridegroom takes the girl to his household, except in rare cases—for example, if he marries an heiress, or if a brother and sister of one family marry a brother and sister of another, with the dowries equal on each side. If a landless wage-worker marries a farmer's daughter, he moves into the house of her parents and into a distinctly unenviable position. He becomes the labourer for the whole family and commands no respect. There is a special term for such people—*nadomnik,* or 'he who gets himself into the house'. In north-east Poland a man in such an arrangement would have to give a dowry and sign a contract saying that his wife had the right to expel him from the house if she became displeased with him. In that case she would have to return his dowry, and give him some alimony.

There are also instances in which a younger son does not inherit the paternal acres, but is paid off by his elder brothers. For him a bride would be sought who is an only child and will bring him both land and goods. About such dowry-hunters the Mazovians have a derisive song:

> *They look for thousands*
> *They have nothing themselves*
> *Comes the wedding day, and*
> *They have to barrow their pants.*

L

The second episode of the marriage drama is the betrothal
—*zareczyny* or *zrekowiny*—solemnized after final agreement
has been reached about the dowry and the wedding outfit.
The prospective bridegroom comes to the cottage of his
bride's parents, preceded by a fiddler. He greets his future
parents-in-law by embracing the knees of each in turn, the
traditional gesture of courtesy and deference. Soon vodka is
set out, supplied either by the parents or the young man, and
all present toast each other.

When all the guests have arrived, the formal act of
betrothal begins, its details following the local custom. It is
directed by the master of ceremonies, known as *starosta*—a
term used to designate a person distinguished by age or by
eminence in any sphere. The *starosta* of the betrothal
ceremony may be one of the original matchmakers, and may
also serve later as master of ceremonies at the wedding.

The young couple place their clasped hands on a loaf of
bread—again the reminder that the agricultural element is
never completely divorced from important peasant ceremonials, and that bread especially is an important symbol in
ceremonial observance as well as in daily living. The
starosta ties the clasped hands together with a long ceremonial
towel; then he cuts the bread and gives each of them half,
thus bestowing his blessing on them.

The ritual completed, the girl's mother brings out refreshments: long, fine noodles with flaxseed oil, cabbage with
peas, rolls, poppy-seed cake made of the finest flour, honey
and other holiday fare.

No special ceremony marks the customary reading of the
banns. There is, in fact, a belief that a girl should not hear
her first banns or her pots will break after she is married.

The next step is the wedding invitations. All relatives and
friends are invited, and in small communities everyone is at
least asked to come and look on, and dance in the yard

outside the house. The invitations are made in person by the bride, who goes from cottage to cottage, accompanied by her maid of honour, the *druzka*. On entering she greets the household with the customary 'Praise the Lord!' Then she goes to each person in turn, beginning with the head of the house and continuing in order of seniority, bends down to embrace their knees and says, '*Prosze na wesele*'—'Pray come to my wedding'. During her first 'bow' the bride may be presented with small gifts for her future household.

As the wedding day approaches, feverish activity seizes the home of the bride. Every alcove, nook and corner is thoroughly scrubbed and whitewashed. Several days before the wedding the bride's mother goes to those women of the village who are happy in marriage, and asks them to come and mix the dough for the cake. The baking of the huge round wedding cake, known as *korowaj*, is one of the most important of the wedding rites, participated in by many people and highly significant for its portents of the future.

When the invited *korowajczynie*, gather in the cottage, the bride's mother receives them with warm hospitality, serving them vodka with tempting snacks and sweets—sausage, ham, pickles, little pies and cakes. Having eaten, the honoured bakers set themselves to mixing the dough. It is made of wheat-flour, without salt in order that the life of the young pair may contain only sweetness. The process, like the cake itself, has symbolic significance. If the cake rises well, things look promising for the future of the bride and groom. Only women are supposed to be present, except for the matchmaker, or *swat*.

The separate troughs of dough are pieced together to make the mammoth cake, on which are moulded symbolic decorations. Chief of these are the moon and sun, representing the bride and groom. When the cake is ready in all its hugeness and splendour, it is placed on an enormous shovel and put into the oven. Then begin a series of antic dances—with the shovel, with the mixing trough, the women laughing, making faces, jumping about, and kissing each other gaily. The lone male among them tries to make his escape but they catch him and kiss him soundly, 'so that the *korowaj* won't throw itself about in the oven'.

An old wedding song tells that sometimes the *korowaj* was so large it could not be taken out, and rather than break it they would tear the oven down. It has to be large, since it is the principal wedding cake and there must be more than enough for everyone present. Pieces will be saved and taken to relatives who could not attend the wedding, and whatever is left will be given to the children. The bottom of the *korowaj*, known as *podeszwa*, sole, is made of rye and is reserved for the musicians.

The evening before the wedding is called the 'maiden evening' or *dziewiczy wieczor*, and usually this is the night for the 'unbraiding' of the bride's hair. The unbraiding ceremony is supposed to be solemn, and at one time it undoubtedly was. A girl who had lost her virginity might be so overawed by the impressive preparations that she would confess to 'having been to the nettles'. In such a case there would be no unbraiding for her, just as there is none for a widow who marries again. Today, however, the unbraiding has lost its solemnity and is likely to be very gay, with comic songs and broad jokes.

All the bridesmaids and friends of the bride gather at her home and sew or make decorations, to the accompaniment of traditional songs bidding farewell to her who will leave their group the next day. The men join them later, after a 'bachelor' gathering of their own.

For the actual unbraiding a special seat is prepared, the

wooden bread trough is placed on the floor bottom up, and over it is spread a white cloth or a fur coat—with the fur to the outside, because that means prosperity. The preparation of the seat varies considerably. In one locality a cross is placed on the table and a loaf of bread is put in the trough, which is covered first with its own wooden top and then with a white cloth, on which a pillow is placed. The bride is seated on her impromptu throne while the other girls bind her braid tightly, studding it with pins to make the process of unbraiding as long and difficult as possible.

Next comes the bargaining for the braid, between the groom or his representative as buyer and the bride's brother or some close kinsman as seller. The bargain completed, the bride's salesman accepts the money and the purchaser is privileged to undo the 'obstacle' braid. Finally the salesman proclaims the unbraiding ended, all offer gifts, and the salesman ties the ribbon from the braid to the bridle of his horse, as a sign that his sister has preserved her virtue to the last.

An interesting additional feature of the 'maiden evening', practised in some parts of Poland, is the 'buying of the wreath', the symbolic significance of which parallels that of the unbraiding. The elaborately prepared 'wreath' which will be featured on the wedding day, is in fact no wreath at all, but more like a bouquet, sometimes fastened on a stick. Nevertheless, in word and in thought it is equated with the wreaths that maidens wear and married women do not. It is made of green leaves, studded with apples and sweets. The plants used in it are those whose leaves do not lose their green even in winter—rosemary and especially the hop vine, a plant cherished above all others by country girls. They cultivate it in their gardens and the expression *siac rute*, to sow the hops, means to be marriageable.

The purchaser of the wreath is generally the best man, or *druzki*, assisted by one of the matchmakers. The *druzki* is the chief support of the groom as the *druzki* or maid of honour is of the bride. When the bargain has been struck, the bride-groom pays the money to one of the bridesmaids, who as a rule hands it over to the bride. But it is a cause of real pride and gloating if the *druzki* succeeds in stealing the wreath beforehand, and making off with it.

The use of the wreath in Polish wedding ceremonies dates far back, perhaps to pre-Christian times. As a symbol of virginity and maidenly beauty it represents one of the ele-ments in the marriage agreement. In everyday speech, especially among peasants, virginity is called 'wreath'. If a girl dies while she is still a virgin, it is said that 'she died in the wreath'. In folksongs the maiden's wreath appears almost as a living creature, all make way for it and bow their heads.

> *There goes the wreath, from the alcove to the door*
> *Mary, fall at your parents' feet, drop down*
> *The wreath goes from the alcove to the room*
> *Step aside, people, let it not be crowded.*

It appears also as a symbol of lost happiness:

THE GIRL: '*Oh, the unhappy verandah where I lost my wreath!*'

THE BOY: '*If it were not for this verandah, my dear girl,*
      You would have your wreath, my dear girl, tra-la-la.'

And again:

> *Damn you, you soldier! The Lord will punish you for me*
> *You took my wreath, and now I'm ugly*
> *You took my wreath, so take me too*
> *My dear little Mother won't have me without my wreath.*
> *You took my wreath, so take me too*
> *Without my wreath I am an orphan!*

At last the wedding day itself arrives. It is a day crowded with activity and with emotions, constantly alternating between grief and joy, solemnity and clowning. Early in the morning relatives begin to appear at the bride's home and neighbours, bridesmaids, ushers, all gather for the breakfast. They are greeted at the door by music and singing. If a beggar should come on this day he too will be welcomed and fed, so that the young people may have a happy life.

The first guest to arrive will also affect their future. If it is a man the husband will rule the household, if a woman the wife will be dominant. In the course of the breakfast the bridesmaids and the more important older women sing various wedding songs, the maidens expressing regret over the bride's abandonment of the wreath. To the accompaniment of these songs the bride bids farewell to the home of her birth, to the threshold and the hearth, and asks her parents for their forgiveness and their blessing.

At the word that the groom's party is approaching, the family of the bride sets about placing obstacles which must be overcome before the young man can gain entrance to the cottage. Sometimes a gate of sticks or poles is constructed at the entrance to the bride's home. With the two parties ranged on opposite sides of the barrier, a mock rebuff is staged. The bride's defenders ask, 'What travellers are these, from what country are they? Whence doth God bring them? What do they want here? Are they after some purchase? What sign have they?'

One of the matchmakers steps forward and pretends to display some sort of papers, but occasionally the defenders are adamant and the groom's party resorts to force. More often, however, a flask of vodka buys them admission.

When the groom's party finally enters the cottage, after all these trials, it is greeted at the entrance by music. The groom, however, does not enter until the bride herself comes to the door and bows to him.

The bridal couple now perform the ceremony of walking around the table 'following the sun', and the bride kisses the loaf of bread on the table, weeping as she does so. Having circled the table, the two stand behind it for that indispensable feature of the wedding, the oration. Delivered by the best man or the master of ceremonies, this address is intended to interpret the significance of the event and the behaviour of all concerned. The symbolic wreath purchased the night before is conspicuous, for this is the occasion on which it is formally relinquished.

Stanislaw Dworakowski, a young Polish ethnographer, took down an oration given at a wedding in a village not far from Warsaw, in 1935:

'I stand as an assistant before this large assembly of wedding participants and guests, gathered to witness this act of marriage. With this green wreath I greet the bride and the bridegroom and all the assembled company. I see this group surrounding the bridal pair who are presently to appear before the priest to perform the holy act of marriage.

'Now the time has come for the groom to give the wreath back to the bride in token of unsullied love from this day forward until the end of life. May this love never be broken, but remain indivisible as your hands joined together today by the priest. We see this wreath in the hands of this respected youth. Like the sun marching across the heaven is this proud wreath, a worthy part of the marriage act.

'Look at the wreath, oh maiden! It is vanishing from your sight, like a bird that wings aloft in the sky and is soon lost to view. Speak to it: I have worn thee from infancy until this day. Now I lose you, and never again shall I return to maiden virtue. Now I beg the forgiveness of my dear parents and ask for their blessing! Father and mother, bless your children!'

The orator now turned to the groom's attendants and spoke for the groom:

'I thank you, noble squires, whose companionship I have had since my earliest years. I am now leaving your midst, I

shall no longer frequent the places where I have been wont to
go. I thank you, noble squires, for all your efforts and your
trouble, I shall never be able to repay you except by this
bow, and by my humblest thanks.'

He addressed the bride's parents, and then the maid of
honour:

'Father and mother, bless them now, before the priest ties
their hands. Maiden, take thou this verdant wreath.'

With these words, the speaker handed the wreath to the
maid of honour, who replied in the following roughly
rhymed and metred words:

> Gladly and humbly I accept this wreath
> From the hands of the bridegroom and his best man
> I know not myself what herb is in it
> That makes the groom a friend of the bride.
>
> Sir Bridegroom, look not at other maidens now
> For the time has come when you must vow to one alone.
>
> For the red flower, for the green wreath
> I thank the bridegroom and his best man.

After the exchange of speeches, the apples and sweets with
which the wreath is studded are removed, and each receives
his share. One of the older women takes a switch—or in some
regions the wreath itself—and strikes the bridesmaids and
unmarried groomsmen over the head, admonishing them to
marry:

> Bachelors—youths and maidens!
> Pray to God to sprinkle you
> With heaven's dew
> That you may not sit until your hair is gray
> For there is nothing worse
> Than to be a bachelor or maid
> When your hair is gray.

The refreshments and speeches disposed of, all prepare for
the journey to the church. The cottage becomes a hive of
activity. The softer-hearted among the womenfolk weep,
others sing departure songs as the wagons which will carry

the company to church line up in front of the cottage. In the mountain regions, the entire party goes to church on horseback.

Just before the departure, the bridal pair once more ask their parents' blessing, and beg from their relatives and friends a 'good word' that will bring them luck. The girl leans her head against the stove, which represents the ancestral hearth—the hub of household activity—and she must be dragged away from it by force.

In some places the moment of leaving has its special observance. One form is that after everyone is seated in the wagon, the bride's mother—dressed in a sheepskin coat worn inside out, symbolizing riches—runs across the road three times, her footsteps imprinting the form of a cross. Or the best man, led by the musicians, walks three times around the wagons, sprinkling them with holy water.

This solemn moment over, the procession sets off with noisy cracking of whips, stamping of hooves, and general outcries. The bells on the harness jingle, the musicians play, the boys shout above the singing of the girls. The bride keeps looking backward, so that her girl-friends may marry soon. Her parents leave the gate wide open after the wagons have rolled out, so that happiness may freely follow their daughter. The mother may throw oats on the bridal couple, and the wedding guests wheat and peas, 'so that their offspring may be as many as peas in a pod'. As they ride through the village the wedding guests call out: 'We ask for a good word! Please, a good word!'

Arriving at the church, the party arranges itself for the march to the altar. The best man steps forward, lays on the altar a 'twist' of wheaten bread called *kolacz*, and lights a candle beside it. Behind him comes the master of ceremonies bearing the ring or the wreath on a tray.

The bride kneels at the left of the groom—if possible on the tail of his coat, for this will give her the dominant role in the household. She also may try to be first to set foot on the altar steps, for this too can determine who rules the household.

After the wedding ceremony, the party usually stops at the first tavern 'for honey'. Here a reception for the entire village may be held, since the cottage would hardly accommodate so many people. The refreshments are contributed jointly, the men paying for the liquor and the women supplying *pierogi*—the popular filled pastries, in crescent shape. It is the pleasant duty of the best man to make sure that everyone is treated to vodka. And all sing:

> *Hey, up to the table, gentlemen! Up, company*
> *We shall pay for the honey and the wine*
> *Together we shall pay for the honey and the wine.*

On returning to the bride's home, the wedding party is greeted at the door by her parents, holding out, on the cover of the bread trough, vodka, bread and salt. The couple drink the vodka, eat a morsel of the bread, and lay a coin on a plate held by the mother. Greeting the newly-wed pair with bread and salt is common throughout Poland, although today most of the charming customs formerly connected with the ceremonial have disappeared. A song usually accompanies the greeting:

> *Mother, spread linen*
> *From the corner to the threshold—*
> *Your children are coming!*

As at several other points during the ceremonies, it is a matter of moment whether the bride or the groom crosses the threshold first, for this will determine who rules their future household. The bride tries hard to be first but the best man is on guard and if he sees her manoeuvre will call out, 'Foot back, please!'

Seating the company at the wedding feast is an important and delicate affair, planned and managed by the best man or the master of ceremonies, with careful observance of seniority and status. The groom's retinue ask for the places of honour: 'Our company comes from afar, we ask you to give us the honour seat at her father's table.' The bride's companions answer, 'Slowly now, don't break the table *and* the honour places!'

The success of the marriage is thought to depend in large measure on the sumptuousness, lavishness, and above all on the gaiety of the wedding feast. A proverb says: '*Jakie wesele, takie i pozycie*', like wedding, like life. The music must no* stop for so much as an instant, and to prevent any break, the bridesmaids put morsels of food into the mouths of the players, so that they will not need to take their hands from their fiddles.

The younger guests are carried away by the music. New songs are improvised for the occasion, the boys vying with the girls, and when a particularly successful song is evolved the others take it up and sing in chorus. During the meal the groom's attendants, who bring the food to the table, dance with the various dishes before they serve them, to insure prosperity to the bridal pair.

Among the foods traditionally part of the wedding feast are peas, *kasha,* or buckwheat, often prepared with gravy, meat and mushrooms, a hen or cock. When the soup is served—the sour beet soup, *barszcz* or cabbage soup, *kapusniak*—the guests cry out, 'The soup is bitter, bitter!' until the bridegroom conquers his shyness and kisses the bride. More important are the flat, braided 'twists'—*kolacze*— which represent all bread and command the veneration always attached to it:

> Kolacz *is the base of everything*
> *And one may say with confidence*
> *Without it, it's as if there were no wedding—*
> *It's like no wedding without it.*

A dance with the *kolacz* blessed at the church is one of the traditional features of the wedding, after which it is ceremoniously shared and eaten by all present.

Equally important is the huge wedding cake, the *korowaj*. The first and the last bite of it are eaten jointly by the bridal couple, and sometimes they carry pieces of it, tucked inside their blouses, all through the wedding ceremony as a charm against evil powers.

Until rather recent years, a very important feature of the wedding ritual was the *pokladziny*, literally the 'laying down' of the bridal couple—escorting them to their room and putting them to bed. Today the name and the ceremonial are preserved among some of the country people as an echo of a once national custom. Where the ceremony exists at all it is in greatly reduced form and often has slipped to the level of a lusty joke.

In one region the wedding dignitaries lead the young couple to the room where a pallet has been spread for them on the floor, made of straw and a few thorns 'lest the husband and wife stay too late abed in their life together'. For pillows they have two loaves of bread and a bottle of vodka. Standing by the door of the bridal chamber the guests sing appropriate, if not always prudish, good-night songs and then go to their own beds to renew their vigour for further festivities.

Their withdrawal gives opportunity for young men who were not invited to the wedding, but hang about as onlookers, to play pranks on the sleeping and often tipsy guests. They sew clothing together, hide parts of it, transfer household dishes or furnishings to strange places and then collect rewards for helping to find them.

A custom formerly connected with the 'laying down' but now almost extinct, was the announcement to the assembled company on the wedding night of the bride's virginity, or her lack of it. The announcement of virginity set off a burst of pride and jubilation. But if the case were otherwise, unpleasant demonstrations followed. A straw wreath and a black kerchief were hung on the cottage, and straw yokes were put around the necks of the bride and her attendants. Her mother was made to drink from a leaking pot and dishwater was poured over her. If the groom confessed that the fault was his and begged forgiveness, the recriminations ceased, but all festivities ceased also.

The capping ceremony, *oczepiny*, follows the wedding night and marks the initiation of the novice into the sisterhood of married women. It also marks the full acceptance of the husband's role and rights. The bride seeks to defer this decisive capitulation as long as possible. She struggles to defend herself, tries to throw off the cap, and when finally subdued submits with louder weeping and lamentation than for the marriage itself.

The once popular custom of cutting the bride's hair as part of the capping ceremony—or sometimes as part of the unbraiding—has survived only in a few regions. Formerly, in Poland as elsewhere in Europe, girls wore their hair uncovered in braids and married women had shorn locks tucked under a cap. Among the mountaineers, the bride's hair was fastened to the threshold and the groom severed it with one stroke of his axe while whirling in a dance, thus giving proof of his dexterity and strength. For the most part, however, the act of cutting was more sedate if no less ceremonious.

Today, a token wisp may be cut off, or none at all. Even today, however, there is a distinct difference between the coiffure and headdress of married women and of girls. In some places, married women do wear caps, even though their hair is not cut, each region having its own distinctive style of cap. Where they do not wear caps, they still are apt to cover their heads with a kerchief when they go out. The dressing of their hair is far less elaborate than that of young girls, and they are apt to wear it up on their heads while girls often wear their braids hanging. The elaborate head-dresses in which Polish peasants of both sexes delight are for unmarried girls, not for married women. The bride would wish to wear at her wedding the most ambitious headdress of her whole life. It will be in the shape of a wreath or crown, streaming with coloured ribbons, loaded with flowers, feathers, beads, in profuse array. From that day on she will never wear a wreath, or any fancy headdress—unless she is the kind of woman who would flout the local mores and bring down on herself criticism and suspicion.

Thus, although the capping ceremony has changed, its basic fact remains—that when a girl marries, she transforms the arrangement of her hair and the covering of her head. It is almost as if the visible seat of maidenhood or matronhood were the top of the head—a localization not special to Poland as witness the recent shaving of the heads of French and Italian girls suspected of consorting with Nazis. Formerly it was customary for Polish peasants to shave the head of a 'fallen woman' and lead her through the village with a halter.

One version of the capping ceremony begins with a song:

> *Not the wedding this,*
> *But the capping rite*
> *Not a maiden this,*
> *But a matron this.*

Throughout the ceremony the bridesmaids and the matrons sing in opposition, the maids mourning and resisting the loss of their companion, and her loss of girlish preroga-tives, while the matrons insist on and rejoice at her entrance into their ranks. One of the bridesmaids' songs has many stanzas, each sung by a different girl, with the last two and the refrain sung by all in chorus. As the mournful melody is

sung, the bride and her former companions kiss each other
and weep:

> *Dear young woman, you will have to change your life*
> *Now you will be a pretty housewife*
> *You will have the keys in your hand*
> *And you will take care of everything, day and night.*
>
> *But listen to my advice*
> *If you would always be in the right*
> *Love your husband deeply and faithfully*
> *Carry out his wishes to the dot*
> *Be stern and friendly with your household*
> *That they may look up to you as a good mother.*
>
> *When you wake up in the morning*
> *Make haste to rise*
> *Thus setting an example for your household*
> *And get to your tasks as quickly as you can. . . .*
>
> *Whatever the Lord gave you, be thankful for it*
> *Do not show your teeth in vain—*
> *If you feel like quarrelling*
> *Fill your mouth with water.*
>
> *Already you have forsaken us*
> *And will go to your husband's parents*
> *You leave behind your mother, who fed you until now*
> *You are no longer a virgin.*
>
> *No more will you adorn the Holy Images with us*
> *And no longer will you bear the white flag*
> *Harden your heart to misery*
> *You will have to bear injustice from strangers.*
>
> *And when snow covers our fields*
> *No longer will you spin with us*
> *No longer will you sing merry songs*
> *Or amuse your bridesmaids with tales.*
>
> *No more will you dance with us*
> *Neither at spinning evenings nor at harvest time*
> *You will have to look after your household*
> *And take care of the babies.*

Presently the married women sing a far more cheerful
version of what is taking place, while a 'dresser' removes the
bride's wreath and puts on a cap of the type prescribed by
local custom. Three times the bride, weeping and protesting,

THE 'LAJKONIK' CELEBRATION IN KRAKOW

DANCING 'KRAKOWIAK'

throws off the cap, until at last the groom himself puts it on her and declares that it looks entrancing. Then the married women, *swaki*, clap hands and cry, 'The bride is ours!' while the bridesmaids still insist, 'Ours!' The bride herself complains,

Like a lily yesterday—
A frightful hag am I today.

Her outcry is a vital part of the ceremony. If she offered no resistance, people would say in disgust, 'She can't wait'. Her bridesmaids sing:

My lavender wreath, fall not from my head
For with my own little hand have I woven thee
While yet a maid.

Perhaps the most popular song in all the wedding festivities is an ancient song about the hopvine, known all over Poland. It is sung by the married women during the capping ceremony and originally had sexual connotations, although today it is thought of simply as a ritual song:

You, Hopvine, if you had not climbed the pole
You would not have made women out of maidens
Oh Hops, Oh my poor one
Up again, down again
Poor Hops!
But you, Hops, climbed the pole
You stole a wreath from all the maidens
Oh Hops, Oh my poor one.
Up again, down again
Oh Hops, my flourishing plant
We couldn't have wedding without you,
Oh Hops, Oh my poor Hops!
Up again, down again—
Oh Hops, you thief,
You robbed the maiden among the sunflowers.

It is still customary to take up a collection 'for the cap' on behalf of the bride. The older women go about among the guests, singing:

A gift for her cap the young bride asks
Willingly she wears it on her head
Quickly now, let none his gift withhold
Lest the young bride's head be cold.

M

The resistance displayed by the girl at various points in the courtship and marriage ceremonies is highly formalized, and it would be considered unbecoming for her to welcome her new status without a show of protest and lamentation. Nevertheless it is likely that some of the tears are genuine. A girl has reason to feel strong conflict about the change symbolized by putting off the maiden's wreath and covering her hair with a matron's headgear.

On the one hand, marriage is the career to which her whole training and ambition have been shaped. It represents fulfilment and not to achieve it would spell public failure. The marriage ceremonies are her high spot of triumph and glamour. The bride is the centre of attention. Dressed in finery which in itself delights her, she is pampered and praised, all the elaborate festivities revolve about her. This is literally the time of her life.

Yet the poetry of the bridesmaids' mournful song surrounds a bitter core of fact. 'After the wedding,' an old woman summed it up, 'hard life begins for the bride. She is put to work immediately and ordered about by her mother-in-law. She will never again dress up her hair and never again go out. From now on, she is someone's property.'

Technically she is in fact the property of her husband and he generally exercises his authority physically as well as morally. Wife beating is the rule rather than the exception—'If you don't beat your wife, her liver starts to rot.' It should be added that husband beating, though not sanctioned by proverb, is also a commonplace.

When they go to church the woman walks a little behind her man, and when they arrive there the women sit apart. There is even a tendency to speak of women as if they were not quite people. In describing a gathering, if one says 'people were there' it means that men only were present. Otherwise one would say, 'people were there and also women!' According to a popular proverb, 'A hen is not a bird and a woman is not a human being.'

To some extent the male dominance is more formal than functional. The peasant places great value on his wife's opinions and is reluctant to act without her counsel. The ideal wife is clever enough to advise her husband well and to see trickery where he might miss it. She is also, of course, sublimely self-sacrificing. Polish folklore abounds in tales of women sacrificing themselves for family or for country, the arch-type being the beautiful Queen Jadwiga who renounced her own love for the sake of her country and her God.

In a sense the peasant regards his wife more as a mother than as a sex mate. The most rigorous restraint is imposed on references to sex after marriage, and it would be indecent for husband and wife to see each other naked. For young people there is no limitation on sex allusions and jokes, but with married people custom forbids sexual reference or even expressions of affection. A kind word between them is considered not quite nice. A young man is on equal footing with his fiancee and may even show her a certain chivalry. But when he becomes her husband he becomes her superior, her master, her owner. Custom says that a kind intention must be masked by a hard word.

The mother role in a number of ways does carry compensating elements, one being respect. The veneration accorded to the Virgin Mary extends in some measure to all mothers. A man may feel that he has too much respect for his wife to regard her as an object of sexual excitement. In speaking of his wife to others, a man uses his own name plus the suffix *owa*, meaning 'wife of'. He avoids using her given name even before their children, as that would be disrespectful. After she is thirty-five and has become a mother, he usually addresses her as *stara*, which means old one. In front of the children he calls her 'mother'. The wife may call the husband by his first name, or address him as 'father', but women are usually more relaxed in these formalities. She may even add a warm word occasionally in speaking to her husband.

The woman has also a limited sphere of independence, which she may manage to extend. In strictly household matters her rule is underwritten by the force of the proverbs: 'The woman keeps three corners of the hut and the man only one'; and again, 'As long as the man does not invade the pots, everything goes smoothly in the house.' This authority does not extend to family affairs. The husband can exercise sole sway in serious discipline of the children and decisions about inheritance or marriage settlement.

The woman's sphere includes the dairy and the vegetable garden which she plans, plants, and tends. Such independence as she has is reinforced by her right to keep for her own what she receives for vegetables, butter, and eggs sold at the fair. That she manages to retain a good deal of spirit is suggested by the proverb: 'There is no power can keep a *baba's* tongue behind her teeth.' Yet each woman must win her own measure of autonomy against the pattern set up by the accepted forms, and not all succeed in the struggle. It is not surprising therefore if the bride is torn between the triumph of finding a husband and a household on the one hand, and on the other reluctance to enter a new role which will be difficult if she plays it successfully, and otherwise will be intolerable.

The final act of the wedding ceremonies is the removal— *przenosiny*—when the young matron leaves the home of her parents and goes to live with her husband. *Przenosiny* may come several weeks after the wedding, but it is always carried through with flourish. Once more there are farewells, blessings, 'good words' and appropriate songs.

A leading theme of the songs is the proverbial struggle

between the bride and her new mother-in-law. 'They will quarrel over anything, but chiefly over who will have the key to the larder—even though the larder may be empty.' A popular song says:

> *No good person should ever be a mother-in-law*
> *For a husband's mother is like a stinging nettle*
> *The stinging nettle can be used for a fence*
> *But there's no way of pleasing the mother of one's man.*

The bride repeats and intensifies her show of resistance during the removal ceremony. Sometimes the groom has to carry her to the wagon in his arms. Sometimes her parents join in and put up barriers to keep their daughter from leaving just as on the wedding day. It goes without saying that the struggle ends in victory for the groom.

While the boys load the chests and boxes containing the bride's trousseau on to the wagon, they groan and complain about the tremendous effort, indicating that the trousseau is very rich. In reality it often is very heavy, weighted by bolts of homespun linen—and, occasionally, by rocks that the untiring practical jokers have stuffed into the trunks beneath the finery and household goods.

The journey to the new home is paved with omens of the young couple's future life. If the horses drawing the bride's trousseau snort, the pair will prosper. If the horses should break loose and run away, the bride will leave her husband and run back to her parents. If by some mischance she tears her dress, the marriage will break up.

The wedding of a widow or widower is much simpler than a first wedding. Their is no *korowaj*, the bride has no bridesmaids, and wears a kerchief on her head instead of a wreath.

In recent times weddings have become less elaborate for all, perhaps chiefly because the modern tempo forbids feasts that last for several days. Accordingly, various types of

wedding will be found in the same region, adapted to the
means of the family. There are, for example, weddings known
as 'mounted', *konne*, with music, *grane*, or 'in a bag', *we
worku*. In the 'mounted' weddings, which are more and
more rare, all the men in the party ride horseback; weddings
'with music' are the most frequent and generally last two
days. Weddings 'in a bag' are the simplest, without music,
with little beyond the marriage ceremony, and with so few
guests that 'the whole thing could be put in a bag'.

> *In olden times when young ones married*
> *The wedding lasted two weeks*
> *Now, the moment they are joined*
> *The wedding is over.*

THE HOUSEHOLD

When the bridal pair arrive at their new home, they are
greeted with bread and salt, or with bread and honey 'so that
their life may be sweet'. The custom gives literal backing to
the name *miodowe miesiace*, honey months or honeymoon.

The bride, who has just taken leave of her own family
hearth, is led to the stove in the new home by her mother-
in-law, a formal introduction to the hearth that will now be
hers. It is a significant moment for both women. As suggested
by the final wedding songs, there is proverbial conflict with
the mother-in-law over who 'has the keys to the larder', that
is the real *gospodyni*, or mistress. Sometimes the young
couple live with the husband's parents, and quarrel with
them. For the most part the husband takes his wife's side and
after they have a child—especially a son—her position will
be stronger. If the relationship with the in-laws is difficult
the young couple may build a house of their own. Or if the
parents have retired, they may gradually be pushed out. But
obviously the honey-months carry their quota of gall for all
concerned.

The great stove to which the bride is introduced is literally as well as symbolically the hub of household activity. Built into a corner, it occupies about one-third of the room and serves as furnace, stove, and in some localities as a sleeping or resting place. It is made of whitewashed brick with iron grills on which the cooking pots are set. Its ample top offers to the very old and the very young a bed, or a place where they can sit in warm comfort. To say that a person is on or behind the stove means that he enjoys security, ease, and freedom from responsibility. This is the meaning conveyed by the familiar saying, 'He lives like one behind God's stove.'

Like any wood-burning fireplace, the stove requires constant tending, and this is a large order since it is kept burning most of the time. As centre and symbol of the home it is regarded with affection and treated with respect—but for all the honour it enjoys, it is not immune from invasion by roaches.

The room in which the huge stove occupies a commanding position is the one in which the real living of the family is done. Poor cottages have only this room with perhaps a smaller one behind for sleeping. The most characteristic Polish peasant cottage, however, has two rooms separated by a corridor that also serves as a store room for farm implements. The 'white room' is reserved for special occasions— entertaining guests or celebrating family festivities. The other is the 'black room' where the family eat, sleep, cook, work, and where the poultry and baby livestock join them during hard winters.

The room must be large to accommodate so much activity. Its walls are covered with whitewash, renewed once a year, or for special occasions like a wedding. It has a low, beamed ceiling and small windows which are seldom opened for fear of cold and fever. Even on the hottest summer days the windows are kept tightly closed and the air becomes so thick 'you can hang a hatchet on it'. Because the windows are so small the room is never bright, even at high noon. At night it is dimly lit by an oil lamp which becomes a centre of activity when there is indoor work to be done.

The simple wooden furniture is often home-made—a long table with benches that are pushed against the wall when not in use, a few chairs perhaps, some small stools, cupboards for the dishes and pots. The gaily decorated hope chest is usually kept in the white room. It holds the holiday clothing and other household treasures, as well as the dowry of the daughters, stored in it piece by piece. Its bright colours contrast with the dark simplicity of the other furniture which in most places is undecorated. In the mountain regions, however, where everything is more highly ornamented, the furniture is often carved with intricate designs.

The beds are made of wooden planks set on short legs. They are wide enough for several people and are usually filled to capacity. It is almost unheard of for a Polish peasant to sleep alone in a bed. Little children are put in rows at the bottom of the bed. Straw-filled mattresses laid on the planks are not the acme of downy softness, even for solo sleeping, and the children often prefer to lie on the benches along the wall, or behind the stove with their grandparents. The young people may prefer to sleep in the barn or, during the summer, out in the open.

An unusually prosperous family may have one or more additional rooms for sleeping. In an average family, if it is a large one, some may sleep in the 'white' room.

The differences between the homes of the poor and the prosperous are comparatively slight, just as are the differences in their daily work routine. More prosperous families will have more handiwork, especially embroidery, displaying the skill and industry of the marriageable daughters. One index of opulence is the pillows arranged in neat piles on the chief bed, which may be for show rather than for use. They should be piled high on top of each other, the smallest on top. Covered with white linen and strips of lace through which gleams the red of the pillow, they add a colourful and lively touch. The more pillows, the richer the home.

Each house has an 'honorary corner', opposite the stove. Here hang the holy pictures of the saints, always including the Virgin Mary. The corner is decorated with flowers and green boughs for holidays, and with souvenirs of pilgrimages to the holy cities. Candles are lighted before the various pictures at the appropriate times. At certain seasons the cottage blooms with the bright, vari-coloured paper cut-outs that contribute to the holiday festivities.

As in so many aspects of Polish peasant life, the cottages show not only regional differences but also marked individual variations within each region. The arrangement of furniture and household goods is far less conventionalized than in the urban United States, for example. A burglar would have more trouble in Poland than in New York City to find what he wanted—even if the family were rich enough, as few Polish peasant families are, to have something he would consider worth stealing.

A moderately prosperous family would have, in addition to the cottage, a barn for storing grain and straw, and a stable for the farm animals. There would also be near the cottage a small garden where the housewife raises vegetables —tomatoes, cucumbers, cabbages, peas, onions. It represents part of her contribution to the family income, since the produce is primarily for sale rather than for consumption, as are the butter she makes and the eggs she gets from the hens.

All these foods are relished, but in a land where almost none escape the pinch of poverty, nobody eats what he can sell unless there is a good reason. Holidays are a good reason, and the gusto with which they are observed may be related to their sanction for throwing over the culinary traces. Sickness is also a good reason, for a sick person cannot work. There is a saying that a Polish peasant will not eat a chicken 'unless he or the chicken is sick'. Eggs and chicken broth are thought to bring strength, and therefore are fed—with whatever regret—to invalids and convalescents. For able-bodied adults they would be regarded as sinful luxuries. Eggs are eaten separately only for special holidays such as Easter or the first day of harvest, and even in cooking they are used sparingly for everyday dishes.

The customary diet is meagre, monotonous, high in starch and low in protein content. Not only does it vary little from day to day, but there is little difference in the three daily meals. The chief variation is seasonal. In winter, food is more scarce, and much use is made of dried or preserved foods—smoked meat or fish, dried mushrooms, legumes, fruits, berries, pickled cucumbers and cabbage.

Despite local variations, peasant fare is essentially the same throughout Poland. Local differences have to do chiefly with supply—for example, fish is an important item in the places where it is available. For the most part, country-folk live on what they raise, eked out by what they can gather in the woods or catch in ponds and streams. Only salt and beverages are commonly bought in shops, and the very poor do not buy even these. They do without coffee and tea, and for seasoning they may use the water from the barrels in which salt herring is kept.

Cooking is long and complicated, requiring numerous utensils and much hovering over the stove, which is kept burning most of the time. Cooking vessels, often made of copper, are cherished and handed down from mother to daughter. Many spices are used, especially dill, poppy seeds and bay leaves. Dried mushrooms do double duty, as food and as flavouring.

In summer the evening meal, eaten when work in the fields is over, is more hearty than breakfast or lunch. At other seasons the three meals are almost interchangeable in size and in content. The stock menu for any meal would be soup and one or more starchy dishes—some form of cereal, potatoes, dumplings, noodles, occasionally *bliny*, the small potato pancakes.

Except on holidays, the main dish is almost invariably one that has to be served in a bowl and eaten with a spoon. According to the season, occasional additions may be made to the menu—such vegetables or fruits as were not sold, berries, roots or leaves gathered by the women and children.

Although there is scant variety in the foods, there is room for a certain range in flavour through the liberal use of condiments, onions, dried mushrooms and sour milk or cream. The grain dish, often a thick porridge of buckwheat groats, *kasha*, is subject to infinite modification, depending on the resources, imagination and enterprise of the housewife. It may be cooked in milk or water, with or without dried fruits, but more often it is highly seasoned, flavoured with fat, and when possible enlivened with bits of meat, mushrooms or gravy. If one can acquire a scrap of liver to chop into the *kasha* it almost gives the illusion of eating that rare article, real meat. Salt pork is a staple source of fat and of a meat 'effect'. Lard and suet are also used, and a number of vegetable oils—hemp, sunflower, flax and poppyseed.

Potatoes are the twin must for every meal. There will always be either potatoes or some form of cereal, and often both. The potatoes may be boiled, fried, used in soup or pancakes, fried up with salt pork or made into dumplings. They are seldom baked and the skins are not supposed to be eaten, for the skin of any vegetable is 'fit only for pigs'. Dumplings are made of flour, and noodles are popular too, in soup or with meat.

The usual peasant bread is a heavy, sour black rye. Lighter flour is associated with festivity or with opulence. Bread is not to be taken for granted as a regular feature of the menu. In some places it is uncommon and eaten only sparingly. Nevertheless, throughout Poland bread is the revered symbol of all food, and of agricultural plenty. It is, more specifically than other foods, a gift of God and it must always be treated with deep respect. It is kept in a place of honour and must never be set upside-down. To let any food fall on the floor is disrespectful—an insult to God's gift—but this is especially true for bread. If it does fall down one is supposed to pick it up, dust it off reverently, and kiss it, although the rule is not always observed in full. It would also be disrespectful to treat bread like garbage. Any that is not used must be burned.

Some of the ritual loaves are enormous and are moulded into elaborate designs which show distinct regional differences in style. To be competent in baking is indispensable, but to be a virtuoso of the oven is an accomplishment from which a housewife derives pride and praise.

Baking is done in a special tile or brick oven, usually on Saturday as part of the Sabbath preparation. When they put the bread into the oven, the peasant women say, 'In the name of the Father, the Son, and the Holy Ghost' or merely, 'God help'. And they urge, 'Rise, bread, as the sun in the sky!'

The bread trough should not be lent, for 'bread is afraid of the outsider's household'. The importance and the symbolism attached to the bread itself, and to the trough in which it is mixed, have been evident in many of the holiday and marriage ceremonials.

The other dish served as regularly as potatoes or cereal concoctions is soup. The range is extremely wide but by far the best known is beet soup or *barszcz,* served with sour cream like most Polish soups. In summer *barszcz* may be eaten cold, sometimes with slices of hard-boiled eggs, or with a raw egg beaten into it. Cabbage soup, *kapusniak*, is almost as common, cooked alone or with meat stock or bones, and thickened with sour cream. Another favourite is split pea soup with onions and sour cream. On fast days, fish soups are a handy standby—and for the devout Catholic peasants, fast days include not only the seasonal fast periods but also every Friday.

Meat is the peasant's favourite dish. In practice, however, most families can have real meat dishes only on holidays and special occasions. Beef, a prime favourite, is almost never eaten since cows are killed only when they go dry, and calves are sold. Pork, a holiday favourite, is elaborately prepared in a number of ways—boiled in soup, fried, braised, roasted, or pot-roasted after being marinated in vinegar, onions, bay leaves and spices. A traditional Easter dish is sucking pig, elaborately decorated. Cold jellies made of pig's trotters, or the trotters of lambs or calves are also part of the holiday menu.

About once a year the average family kills a pig, creating a dietary high spot and a supply of meat-stuffs that must be stretched as far as possible. When the pig is killed, gifts are sent to the correct recipients, according to established tradition, and each one must receive the correct portion. Hams are cured and smoked, sausages are made, all the parts of the pig's anatomy are used to advantage. The Polish sausages are 'the best in the world' and lend flavour to dishes all through the year, as well as furnishing holiday splurges and occasional snacks. Salt pork is used extensively, and the liver or other organs are chopped up to be miixed with *kasha* or millet.

Although the average peasant so rarely eats a whole piece of meat, he enjoys the taste of meat almost daily. His meat diet is, in fact, chiefly a flavour imparted to cereals and vegetables rather than an intake of protein—a satisfaction of the palate rather than of the stomach.

Fish is eaten much more and enjoyed much less than meat. Fresh fish depends entirely on local supply. Where it is available some will be salted or smoked for winter use.

The vegetables that lend an occasional spice of variety are themselves highly spiced, when they are cooked as a separate dish or pickled for winter use. Often, however, they are made into soups or served with meat. Beets and cabbages are the chief vegetable foods after potatoes. Lettuce, cucumbers and radishes are served raw with sour cream, or lettuce may be wilted and served with a dressing of bacon fat. In recent years tomatoes have become popular, as a raw vegetable or cooked in soup.

Even more welcome as a fillip for the monotonous menu are fruits and berries, eaten fresh in season and dried during the rest of the year. For festive occasions they are baked in pastries, and dried fruits are served as a sweet, almost like candy in the city. Fruit soups, eaten hot or cold, are made of sour cherries or of dried fruits, and are rated almost as desserts. One of many prohibitions against eating foods out of season is the rule that forbids green apples before St. John's, on June 24. Breaking the rule will make a frog grow in the culprit's stomach.

The dairy lends a saving grace to the peasant diet, from the standpoint of health as well as of taste. Fresh milk is more apt to be sold than to be drunk by the family, but sour milk and cream are accessories to innumerable dishes. Potatoes in sour milk are extremely common for breakfast or lunch, sometimes furnishing the sole dish except for soup. Sour cream is used in or on almost anything—soup, meat, potatoes, pancakes, raw vegetables, berries. In the lowlands cottage and pot cheese are very popular, while the mountain region is noted for yellow cheeses called *oszczypki* of incomparable flavour, often beautifully moulded. Some of the ritual cheeses in the mountains are made in the form of animals, as pleasing in shape as they are in flavour.

Butter is more commonly liked than used. Formerly it was liked better aged than fresh, and in some places 'high' butter is still preferred. It is considered the best fat for baking and in general is used for cooking as well as for a spread.

Cakes and pastries are baked chiefly for holidays and important family celebrations. White flour is reserved for party fare, and the more important the occasion the finer the flour. The high, sweet *babka*, rich with butter and eggs, is a favourite, though not a common, Sunday treat for those privileged to enjoy such holiday food on a plain Sabbath, and the higher it rises the prouder the cook. The thin poppy seed cake featured especially at Christmas has been described in some detail. Poppy seeds are popular as filling for pastries at any season, and so are fruits or jams. Typical holiday sweets are an apple-filled pastry called *jablecznik*, and a thin fried dough filled with cheese or jam, known as *nalesniki*. The *pierogi* mentioned as part of innumerable festive meals, are a versatile pastry. Filled with meat or with the many fillings appropriate for Lent and fast days, they are related to the ravioli family. Filled with fruit, they line up with the sweet side of the menu, a cross between a tart and a dumpling.

Honey is served as a party dish, and is also used in cooking. Bees are commonly kept, but wild honey is a prize never to be neglected.

The common beverage is *kvass*, a beer brewed at home from bread. Any good housewife prides herself on making it well. It is drunk more often alone than with meals, and is offered to guests especially in hot weather. She also brews mead from honey, but this is for very special occasions.

Coffee and tea are not very common in the country, especially coffee. They have an aura of luxury that verges on the effete, if not on the dissolute, and are associated with the worthless ways of the city. One of the capping songs instructs the bride:

> *Do not serve coffee at breakfast*
> *This is not fit for the boss*
> *But only for the landlord's cooks*
> *Cook up some water-soup*
> *And serve black bread. . . .*

It goes without saying that no food is wasted. A careless housewife who left food on the plates would be heard after death, scrabbling around in the dishwater for scraps to ease the pangs of her eternal hunger. To do well on little arouses admiration, for anyone can make a good showing if resources are unlimited. There is a sarcastic proverb: 'If a woman has a full larder she's a good housekeeper.' Its meaning is not that a full larder is the sign of a good housekeeper, but that it is easy to win praise if you have an abundance to draw from. A really good housekeeper can serve glorified porridge three times a day and make her family feel well fed.

A good housewife will also keep her family in clean clothes, however limited their wardrobes. The family washing is done about once a week. Dirty clothes are soaked overnight in water that has been treated with ashes from hard wood. Then they are rinsed, preferably near the cottage since one would not want to show them at their dirtiest in public. Next they are folded in layers, each sprinkled with wood ashes, and the whole mass is soaked in boiling water tinctured with steamed wood ash, so that the lye percolates through each layer in turn. Finally the clothes are taken to the stream or river, where they are beaten with wooden paddles, sometimes elaborately carved and decorated. After all this, and after being spread out to dry in the sun, the clothing is snow white and flower fresh. It is the duty of the housewife to provide clean underwear every week and a clean Sunday

shirt for her husband, even if he has to sit shirtless in the
sun or go to bed while she washes it.

Cleanliness of the clothes is more important than cleanliness of the body in the busy household. The concept of
personal hygiene is strict and definite, although by western
standards the hygienic condition in a Polish village presents a
sad picture. The idea of cleanliness, for the Polish peasant as
for many others, is something of an abstraction. When one
sleeps, eats, washes, prepares food for and sometimes houses
domestic animals all in the same room, great fastidiousness is
hardly to be expected.

The peasant makes a great distinction between personal
and impersonal dirt. The dirt that comes from the human
body is repulsive as well as dangerous, and against this he
guards himself. Even the poorest peasant would use different
containers for washing himself or his clothes and for preparing food. There is great disgust for objects intimately
connected with the body. Nobody would pick up a used
handkerchief or a comb lying on the ground. Combs must not
be put on the table and hands should be washed after
touching them.

The washing itself is on the ritualistic side—merely dipping
the hands in water. It is not greatly trusted, however.
Children are taught to avoid touching their genitalia in
bathing, because 'you will eat with those same hands'. The
reason is not fear of germs, but of profaning God's gift.

Everyday washing is limited mostly to putting water in the
hands and rubbing it over the face. During the summer the
soles of the feet are washed, because people go barefoot and
they get very dirty. Older children and youths bathe during
the summer, not for cleanliness but for fun. Grown-ups consider this kind of fun 'improper play'.

Now and then a real bath is taken, in a barrel containing
water heated by hot stones. This must be done in complete

N

solitude since modesty does not permit the members of the family, even the wife or husband, to see each other naked.

The conscientious farmwife must struggle against limitations of time and energy as well as of resources in managing her household. Farm work is proverbially divided so that a large share falls to the woman, and housekeeping must be worked in with tending the garden, the poultry, the dairy—not to mention the babies. An old folk tale, possibly written by a woman, records a complaint that some city wives even in London and New York share with their sisters on the farm:

There was once a man who used to scold his wife for being lazy and not doing any work. At last his wife said to him, 'All right, I will go out to the fields and you stay home and do my work. Then we will see.'

'Good!' said the man, 'I will not only do your work, but I will also find time to sleep.'

'Certainly!' said his wife, 'only don't forget to do everything I do. You have to make the dough for the bread; to make butter; to grind the grain for the soup; to put the soup on the fire and to watch out that the crows don't fly off with the chickens.'

'Fine,' said the man, 'go ahead out to the fields. I will do everything, and I will find time to sleep.'

So his wife went out, and he said to himself, 'It is a waste of time to do everything separately. The best way is to do it all at once, then I will be through and can go to sleep.'

So with one hand he put the flour in the trough and poured water on it; with his other hand he ground the grain for the soup, and with his foot he churned the butter. He went on for some time and got very hot from all the exercise. So he took off his shirt. Soon flies started to bother him terribly. With the hand that was full of dough he reached out for the flies. Soon he himself was full of dough and none was left in the trough. At this moment he heard a hen crying, so he jumped up, overturning the butter churn. But he got out too late—a crow had just taken the last chicken.

When he came back and saw what he had done, he said to himself, 'Oh, what shall I do?' He found no other answer than to hide in a big wooden pail full of feathers. At this moment a neighbour came to the door to speak to his wife. He was so afraid it was his wife that he overturned the feathers and they spilled into the cream set out for the butter. Then there was no place left for him to hide.

Now his wife had finished her work in the fields and came
home. She saw what he had done and she said nothing. But he
said to her, 'Oh wife, never again will I say that you are lazy
and haven't anything to do! And whatever you ask of me now, I
will do it.'
'Fine,' said the woman, 'We will see about that.'

BIRTH AND BABYHOOD

Children are wanted in the Polish peasant home, without
question and without qualification. A woman enjoys greater
prestige in the household and in the community when she
becomes a mother; a man acquires greater status when he
becomes a father. The birth of a child is evidence that God
blesses and approves the parents, and it is viewed as part of
His plan for the world: 'Thus it is and thus it must be.'

About childless couples it is said: 'The Lord does not bless
them with children.' If they are God-fearing and industrious,
their plight evokes sympathy and sad wonder. If their conduct is not beyond reproach, the affliction is viewed as
punishment. The term *przezdzietnica,* or childless one, carries
more contempt than pity.

A childless couple will try to remedy their state by prayer,
fasting, votive offerings, and pilgrimages to holy places, as
well as by medicine and magic. Except for prayer, these steps
are taken by the woman alone, for the peasant believes that
only the woman is sterile.

In spite of the prevailing poverty, there is no fear of large
families. 'God gave the children, He will give for the
children.' If a man owns a sizeable farm, children are an
economic asset, since he will not be obliged to hire paid
labour. If he has only two or three *morgs,* he will count on
feeding his brood by finding work for all hands. And if there
is not enough work at home, he may send one or two out as
paid workers on someone else's farm.

The only exception to the universal desire for children is in the case of an unmarried girl. In most sections an illegitimate child is a calamity and a disgrace, and girls will try to avoid bearing one. The methods of inducing abortion are few, one of them being to induce hemorrhage, even by pricking with a pin; another is to drink a mixture of gunpowder and vodka.

It is taken for granted that parents, especially the father, would rather have a son than a daughter. A son is a 'prop of husbandry', inheritor of property and name, an investment for the future. At the moment of birth it seems to be forgotten that he is also the successor who will displace his father. A daughter, however docile and hardworking, is at best a temporary and expensive acquisition. The marriage of the son will add to the family property but with a daughter 'one must still add something to get someone to take her' and after marriage she is 'a cut off slice of bread'.

The relative evaluation of the sexes is evident in a verse from a wedding oration:

> *If the bride bears a son*
> *The groom will put out a barrel of wine.*
> *But if a daughter*
> *Then only a crust of bread.*

One way of tilting the scales in favour of a son is to put a boy doll or a real baby boy on the bride's lap during the capping ceremony, or when she first arrives in her new home. Omens are carefully watched, and if possible induced. The sex of the first person to enter the home of a newly married couple, or of the first caller on the day before Christmas in a home where a child is expected, will determine the baby's sex, and every effort is made to have the decisive visitor a man. If a child's first word is '*tata*', papa, the next in the family will be a boy; if it is '*mama*' it will be a girl.

In common with other European peoples, both ancient and modern, the peasants believe that a woman who feels and looks well during pregnancy will bear a son and that if she feels miserable, especially if she has yellow spots on her face, the child will be a girl. If the belly is high and round, it will be a boy; if flat, a girl. If the mother feels motion on her right side, it will be a boy: of on the left, a girl.

In speaking of a pregnant woman, one says 'she is in hope'. The treatment she enjoys during pregnancy sharply differentiates that period from the endless round of toil that is usual for the farm wife. The special consideration showered on her is less an expression of concern for her health and comfort than of belief that what she does and how she feels will affect the unborn child. For this reason the various observances and prohibitions are not limited to the advanced stages when special care is necessary, but begin as soon as pregnancy is established.

As pregnancy advances, the husband takes over some of the more strenuous work normally performed by his wife, while other members of the household, or near relatives, help with lighter tasks.

All her whims and desires must be gratified, under penalty of harming the child. Anyone who finds it impossible to grant a pregnant woman's request must throw something at her, or mice will eat his clothing. She must eat well so that the child will grow, but must avoid certain foods—fish, for example—so that the child will not 'swim' in luxury or immorality, or be deaf. She must not eat twin pears, apples, or other fruits, in order to avoid bearing attached twins— even normal twins or triplets are generally regarded as a misfortune. She must not drink out of a chipped vessel or step over an axe, or the child will have a hairlip. And some say she must not eat warmed-over food, or the child will have crooked legs.

The belief that the baby will be marked by what the mother sees is very strong among all classses. She must avoid looking at or touching a dead person, or she may give birth to a corpse, and in any case it will look like a corpse. If she sees a dying animal, the child will suffer from the 'falling disease', epilepsy. She must be shielded from the sight of cripples, and any people or animals that are ugly, abnormal, diseased. If she is frightened by a mouse or rat, the child will have large, hairy moles, known as 'mice'. If she clutches herself in terror at the sight of fire, it will have a red or purple birthmark on that part of its body.

Any work that involves cutting, beating, piercing will cause wounds on the body of the child, so that an expectant mother must not chop wood, wash clothes, or sew. Spinning, plaiting or weaving—which involve knotting and tightening —may cause difficult delivery.

The mother's moral conduct during pregnancy will influence the child as much as will her physical behaviour. She must do nothing wrong; she must not drink or curse or steal or quarrel, nor even take something from a cottage inadvertently, for her conduct will affect her child's character and disposition. Nor must she be sad.

Some prohibitions are designed as protection not of, but against the pregnant woman, who is considered unclean and harmful' until she is purified by the post-natal ceremony of churching. A woman who is 'in hope' must not pick fruit from a tree, or the tree will die. She must not walk across a field, especially a newly sown one, or only weeds will come up. In some regions she is not allowed to hold a child in baptism, for fear harm will come either to her own baby or to the godchild. In others she is not allowed to be matron of honour at a wedding, or the young pair would have a hard life. By popular custom she is not summoned to court or required to take an oath.

The labour of peasant women is generally light and short. Instances of birth in the field, on the road, at the market, are not uncommon. Extensive preparations are made in the hut, however.

As far as possible they are made in secret, to prevent anyone from casting a spell on the mother. The old woman who is to attend her is bespoken in advance, but secretly. Doors, windows and chimney are closed to prevent evil powers from entering, and the bed is curtained off. The men of the household are told to stay away, except the husband, and even he is expected to keep a respectful distance unless he is called to assist. The smaller children are sent to relatives or friends. They are told in advance that the stork brings babies and that their mother is ill because the stork has pecked her.

The old woman, the *babka*, attends the mother during delivery and for a few days after it, performing the duties of midwife, nurse and housekeeper. Later she returns as a conspicuous participant of the christening ceremonies. Peasant women prefer the *babka* to a trained midwife, believing that it is safer to cling to old practices, tested through the centuries, than to seize on new and untried fads.

In olden times the *babka* was supposed to be a person of dignity and position, for it was believed that her qualities would affect the child. She did not receive payment for her services except for ritual gifts of cotton and baked goods. Even today, the baby when it grows older brings gifts to his *babka* during certain holidays, and she enters into a spiritual kinship with the parents. In some places she calls the mother 'grand-daughter' and the father 'grandson'.

If labour is difficult, a variety of means are used to lighten it. The woman may be laid on the ground so that the magical strength of 'the holy earth' will flow into her. All knots in her clothing are untied, all locks and covered chests are opened. In anticipation of this moment, people in some regions warn the bride to see that the garments she wears on her wedding night have no knots tied in them, and when the chests containing her trousseau are brought into the groom's home the lids are left open.

If labour continues difficult, word is sent to have the church door opened, the Holy Sacrament exposed, and the case containing the holy wafers opened. A further treatment is anointing the genitals, or rubbing the abdomen with a mixture of fat and vodka. Blowing into a bottle is a common practice, as are smoking and steaming with a bowl of hot water or burning vodka, or a burning onion.

More drastic methods may be resorted to, if all these fail. The woman is made to jump, or her husband is called in to press on her with fist or knee. If the child is in reverse position, the mother is lifted by the legs and shaken vigorously. In some localities the *babka* will order the husband to bed beside his wife with the words, 'suffer ye both'. This is believed to bring relief to the woman and to ease delivery.

Both the placenta and the navel cord are believed to have magical and medical potency. If a child is 'born in the cap'— covered with a caul—he will be lucky. But one must make sure that the *babka* buries the cap in 'an honourable place' and doesn't steal it for magical purposes of her own. The expression 'born in the cap' is used generally to designate a person who is lucky, though today most people take it as a figurative expression like 'born with a silver spoon in his mouth', and picture a cloth cap rather than the caul.

Some of the beliefs connected with the navel cord are shared by the upper classes, for example, that the number of knots on the cord will determine the number of future births. The object on which the cord is placed after it is cut may determine the future calling of the child. The midwife who attended the birth of Poland's poet-seer, Adam Mickiewicz, is said to have placed his navel cord on a book. For tying, a thread of the female seed fibres of hemp should be used, or the child will be sterile.

The final disposal of the cord may help or harm. If the *babka* steals it she will have power over the baby for the rest of his life. Some hold that if the mother puts the cord on the altar when she is churched, the baby is sure to thrive. Some dry it and use it in powered form as medicine, or the dried cord may be saved and given to the child when he goes to school for the first time, to make him a good scholar. Often it is carried on one's person in later years, for general good luck.

The Poles share the widespread belief in lucky and unlucky birthdays, hours, stars, and phases of the moon. In times of adversity the peasant will exclaim, 'Why was I born in such an unlucky hour?' He accepts quite literally the implications of predestination. Wednesday and Saturday are good days for girls, Tuesday is good for boys. Friday is a day of bad omen for both sexes. A story is told of a man who tried for years to find a wife but all in vain—no girl would have him because he was born on Good Friday.

Unusual markings or features indicate the future fate of a baby. One born with teeth will not live long and some believe that it has two souls, one of which becomes a vampire after death. A baby without eyebrows will also be a vampire, and one born in an unusual position will have 'evil eyes'.

Cripples are regarded as expressions of God's anger and harbingers of misfortune. 'The bald, the squint, the crookshanks are marked out by God.' Accordingly, the congenitally crippled are apt to receive scorn and anger rather than pity and consideration. The afflictions of the blind, the lame, the hunchbacked, the deaf, are invoked as angry epithets with a frequency rather startling among a people not unkind by nature—because the crooked body is viewed as the mark of a crooked spirit, the just reward meted out by God for sin.

The child's first bath is a rite of which every detail must be auspicious—time, temperature, source, vessel, ingredients, disposal. Water for the first bath should not be brought in at sunset, nor should the child be bathed at that time, for this is when evil spirits cast their influence. The boy's bath is heated in a pitcher, the girl's in a pot. In either case the vessel must be new and the water should merely be warmed. If it is brought to a boil the child will be impatient and irritable— one who is 'bathed in hot water'.

The baby is bathed in the bread trough so that it will grow like dough, and everyone entering the house throws into the bath water a few pennies, later taken by the *babka*. Sometimes a gold ring is placed in the bath, so that the child will not be yellow in the face; or a little honey is put into the bath water of a girl so that she may be beautiful and fragrant. Leaves and herbs are widely used. Hazel leaves, so that the child may be strong and walk early, mugwort, artemisia, botony, thyme, all for strength. Some put in lovage so that it will be loved, or milk so that its skin may be white. Bathing in aspen leaves is avoided for they would make its head shake.

If the baby cries and kicks during its first bath it will have a temper but it will also thrive and grow. If it is quiet its disposition will be mild but its chances of survival smaller. In the course of the bath the *babka* 'shapes' the baby's head by gently pressing or rubbing it to induce the roundness that is the peasant ideal. If the head is 'spread' she puts wild flax dipped in white of egg on the forehead, or else 'measures' the head by pressing it gently crosswise and tying it round the forehead.

When the bathing is done, she lifts the baby up three times, saying as she does so: 'Son (or daughter) up, holy water into the ground.' Then she puts a rosary and chaplet around its neck to make sure that it is not a changeling sent by some witch, and holds it out to the parents to kiss, so that they will always have affection for it.

The bath water is carefully disposed of, because it is identified with the child's future and also because the un-baptized baby is unclean. The measures prescribed in different localities are not only diverse but often contradictory, although the reasons for them hold throughout. In some places the water is thrown under the doorstep so that the child may be lucky. In others they pour it where no one walks, so that no one may be harmed by it. Elsewhere it is poured under a sweet pear tree at sunrise.

Formal acceptance of the child into the family circle may be solemnized at the time of the first bath or immediately after the baptism. The baby is placed on the mother's bed, and its pillow is struck with a switch, to the accompaniment of the injunction, 'obey your father, obey your mother!' The other children may also be switched 'until it hurts, so that they may long remember the christening; and the switch is sometimes taken out into the fields 'so that the child may not be afraid of the night'. Later it is hung over the baby's cradle so that he will grow up disciplined and obedient. The switching has been variously explained as exorcising of evil powers, beating for health and strength as in the spring ceremonials, or a symbol of parental authority.

The *babka* continues caring for the child during its first few days, and it is she who swaddles it. The swaddling protects the baby from crooking of the spine, to which Polish mothers think it is highly susceptible. For further protection during this time it is carried about in a long, firm pillow—sometimes by children of the family little older than the infant. More than twice the length of the child, the pillow serves both as mattress and as coverlet. The baby is placed at one end, and the other is folded up covering it to the neck. Then the pillow is firmly tied at the sides and laced over the top.

The baby is kept out of sight as much as possible until it is christened and the mother churched, for during this period it is peculiarly subject to evil powers. It is shown to visitors most reluctantly, and all measures are taken to protect it. In addition to the rosary hung around its neck by the *babka*, various metal objects are used to ward off demons: an axe, a knife, keys. New diapers and clothing are not used before baptism, because they might contain evil, and also might make the child conspicuous.

Any cloths or clothing used for the baby must not be dried outdoors before baptism, as the evil spirits could gain access through them. They must not be fanned by the wind, or the child might be a 'giddy-head'. In some places they must not be wrung or shaken after washing, or he will suffer from constipation. Elsewhere they must not be dried before the fire or the child's clothing will tear all through his life, as if it had been burned.

Especial precautions are taken against the evil eye. Anyone who admires the baby excessively should spit three times and say, 'May the spell fall on a dog'. Otherwise jealous spirits might make the child ugly out of spite.

The general belief in changelings is still firmly held by many. A widely known story tells of a mother who had been nursing a child for five years, but it did not grow. An old beggar woman came by and, recognizing it instantly as a changeling, said: 'Give me an axe, we have to hack this child to pieces.' She laid the child on the threshold and before the eyes of the terrified mother, smote at it. But lo, there under the axe lay a rotten tree stump and in it a nest of snakes. These had been sucking the woman's breast in the guise of the changeling child.

Another story is told of a woman whose child was changed by a witch, but this mother found a way to deal with her. She put the changeling on the doorstep and struck it with a stick, with all her might. The child cried lustily and the witch soon came running, crying out: 'Here, take yours and give me back mine!' And with that she handed the woman's own child back to her.

Though the mother keeps the baby under cover, the joyous tidings travel quickly and people soon come with gifts. Friends and neighbours bring fowl, bread, cheese, eggs, butter, *kasha*, pork fat and honey 'to relieve the sick mistress of household cares' and to furnish a joint feast. The offerings of gifts and food, and the attendant party, take place in some regions a day or two after the birth, or even on the same day, and are often repeated at the christening. The group eating serves as an offering to propitiate evil spirits, and also to enhance fertility, of humans and of fields.

The christening takes place on a Sunday or a holiday, usually within two weeks of birth. If the baby is born on a Sunday, however, it must not be christened on Sunday or it will have the dubious gift of seeing Death when it comes to claim its victims. If the baby looks frail, as if it might not live, it is given 'baptism with water' in its own home, by the *babka* or anyone present, without waiting for the formal church ceremony. For death without baptism would be a major tragedy to the child, the family and the whole community. Formerly unbaptised babies were buried like suicides in the fields or woods, without the usual ceremonies. Their souls are believed to haunt the world in the shape of birds, mice, or shooting stars, begging piteously for baptism. If their pleas go unheeded they bring storms, hail and other disasters. In Silesia the birds that flit about the cemetery-cross on All Souls Day are said to be the souls of unbaptised children, crying for baptism. Whoever hears such a cry should baptize the child with water, saying:

> *If a boy, you are John*
> *If a girl, you are Ann.*

Thereupon the child will stop crying, thank its liberator, and depart, taking with it the misfortunes that come with the unbaptized.

For the church baptism, the choice of godparents is a momentous one. The child's success in life is felt to depend in great measure upon its godparents, since it will inherit their qualities more than those of its own parents. Moreover, the godparents have definite obligations toward the child, and the better their position the more effectively can they sponsor it. In addition, the relationship between parents and godparents is regarded as a spiritual kinship, carrying the privileges and duties of kinship. Therefore it is not lightly given or accepted.

Although the office of godparent involves expense and responsibility, it is seldom declined. To be asked is an honour and to refuse is a sin. If the child died, its death might be attributed to the refusal. Then too, godparenthood increases respect and status, and may bring luck. The person who has never held a child in baptism is looked down upon; in the next world he will 'hold a dog by the tail'.

Both godparents make gifts to the child, but the godmother's is usually the larger: a shirt, a cap and the baptismal cloth. If she fails to give a piece of linen she commits a grievous sin, 'a godmother who doesn't give a shirt or at least a small piece of linen will herself go naked into the next world'.

Small sums of money are also given, known as 'the tie' because the coins are usually tied in the corner of the pillow in which the child is carried to church. The money must not be borrowed or the child will be poor all its life, struggling with debts and never able to make a fortune.

The godparents continue to make gifts to the child when it is small, and occasionally as it grows older. When the godchild marries, financial assistance or at least a substantial gift is obligatory, and they may assume the role of matchmakers.

If the real parents die the godparents are responsible for the child. If the god child dies the godmother sews the shroud and the godfather makes the coffin.

The godparents also acquire a spiritual kinship to each other, and marriage between them is generally frowned upon. It is considered highly auspicious, however, to have godparents who were once in love with each other but did not marry.

The choosing of the name is also a matter for care and secrecy. The most common practice is to give the child the name of the saint on whose day it was born, or on whose day it is baptized, but it may be named for one who is regarded as a special patron of the house or the family. In some regions it is believed that if a saint is favourable to the father he will be well disposed toward the son, who therefore is given the same name; in others, the child is never given the name of a parent, for fear that one or the other will die. The names of brothers or sisters are avoided, since this too would bring death to the child.

In order to outwit the evil spirits, the chosen name is kept secret until the moment of baptism and often is not revealed even to the priest until everyone is in church.

Christening is one of the three most important ceremonials in the peasants' calendar, the others being marriage and burial. Formerly the christening feast was large and lavish, with the entire village attending and several days of feasting and dancing. Recently the celebration has been limited to one day; the guests are usually only the sponsors, relatives and close friends; and there is no singing or dancing unless the party stops at a tavern on the way home from church. As a rule only married people attend, but sometimes musicians are present and there is dancing for everybody.

If the party does stop at a tavern the whole village has an opportunity to learn of the event and share the festivities.

The cost of the tavern refreshments is covered by the sponsors. Stories are told of such hearty celebrations in the tavern that the party failed to get home by daylight and returning late at night, drunk as lords, lost the child on the way.

As the party sets out for the church, they sing:

We take hence a heathen
We shall bring back a Catholic.

In going to and from the church, measures are taken to guard against the evil spirits waiting to pounce on the child—covering its face, or coming back from church at a run. Arriving at the home they sing again:

My dear kinswoman, we are back from church
We took a little Jew, we bring back an angel.

Although the parents stand most of the cost of the christening party, guests, neighbours and friends bring gifts of food. A woman who failed to bring some contribution would be considered lacking in pride or self-esteem. A special cake is baked for the occasion, known as the 'christened doll'. The bigger and better the cake, the better are the child's chances for healthy growth and for success in life. Grain antedated bread as a ritual food, and in many sections the custom has survived of eating a dish of millet seed and honey brought by the *babka,* who receives gifts of money in return.

The drinking also has its ritual aspect. The *babka* goes to each guest with vodka and gives him a small bunch of hops. After drinking, the guest puts some money on the plate for the mother and the *babka.*

The final rite in the birth ceremonies is the churching of the mother, the purification which makes her once more a normal—and a safe—member of society. The origin of this practice goes back to the pre-Christian past, but the Catholic church preserves it in the Feast of the Purification of the Virgin Mary, forty days after Christmas.

The Church regards churching merely as a blessing, and does not class failure to obtain it as a mortal sin. Popular tradition, however, is adamant in viewing the woman as unclean and imposing severe restrictions upon her until she has been churched. The restrictions, like the specific ceremonies, vary from one place to another. In some she is not allowed to work in the fields, for it would be covered with weeds; she may not go to the well for it would dry up or become worm-ridden; she must not milk the cow or attend to any of the livestock. She must not sew or the child will have colic, nor cross the boundary of anyone's land, nor in some places even stand on her own doorstep. She keeps as silent as possible during the six weeks before churching, greeting nobody and avoiding even her husband. A woman who dies before churching turns into a demonic creature called *Mamuna*, who steals healthy children and substitutes her own. She may be buried apart, like a suicide.

The ceremony is simple, and a little lonely in contrast to the prevailing rule of group participation. The mother goes to the church alone, her shawl held over her head, almost concealing her face. The Church does not forbid her to enter, but in many localities tradition does. She must kneel in the entry or in the *babienec* women's section, until the priest has prayed over her and sprinkled her with holy water, after the mass. He holds a candle as he prays, and she touches it. Then she follows him around the large altar, sometimes holding on to his stole to give her a 'lucky hand' or, if the baby is a girl, to give it long hair.

Other ceremonies may be added to the ritual in the church, for example purification by water. In one of these, the mother stands on the spindle on which the child's navel cord was cut, while the *babka* puts some grain on her hands and then pours water on them, over a bowl held by a third woman. The *babka* says, 'I cleanse thy soul from thy sin'. The

o

mother then performs the same ceremony for the *babka*, with the words: 'I cleanse thy hands of my uncleanness'. Then she falls three times at the *babka's* feet and kisses her hands, thanking her for her trouble. After this the *babka* sprinkles the mother and all present with holy water, using blessed herbs as a sprinkler.

The churching is sometimes celebrated by a party at the tavern or by gifts of money, wheat cakes and fowl. It marks the end of the mother's special status as one singled out both for privilege and for avoidance, and the beginning of the baby's acceptance as a regular member of the household and of the community.

From now on, if there is no one to care for the baby at home, the mother will take it to the fields with her. She may improvise a cradle from a sheet slung to a low-hanging branch of a pear or apple tree. Or she may set two sturdy forked sticks in the ground, place a third across them, and hang a sheet from it by the four corners, making a deep hammock into which the child is placed. But she must be careful not to put the improvised cradle on a boundary or near a gateway, where the malign *Boginky* or *Mamuna* could pounce on it.

At home, two forms of cradle are common—one on rockers, set on the floor, or one that hangs from the ceiling above the mother's bed, where she can move it gently with her hand or foot. Whatever the form, the baby will be rocked frequently, for a child is thought to need rocking and some believe that if it is not rocked its head will shake when it grows up. One avoids rocking an empty cradle, however, for that would keep the child from sleping or, some say, give it a headache or even kill it. Moving the cradle is also dangerous for that too might make the child sleepless, or make it cross-eyed when it grows up; and nothing should ever be handed across a cradle.

One never puts a strange child into the cradle of one's own. Even two children of one's own should not be laid side by side in it, for they would rob each other of health and sleep. It is safe, however, to put them in head to tail.

Since parents are eager to have their children grow up as fast and as strong as possible, they take care that nothing is done to hinder growth or injure health. Stepping over a child or young animal is believed to stop its growth, but if one steps back over it immediately the harm is undone. Weighing or measuring will also prevent growth. To call a child a rabbit or frog would have the same effect. In some places one must not even utter the word frog in a child's presence, for it would get a growth under its tongue unless one quickly adds, 'garlic under the child's tongue'.

Children must not look into a mirror or they will become mute like the image; and their hair or nails must not be cut before the age of one year, for fear of sapping the vital powers. Hair-cutting, when done, is accompanied by ceremonies and omens; and care is taken that the severed locks are disposed of in a way that will not harm and may help.

As soon as the child 'moves by itself' the mother stops paying much attention to it, especially if a new infant is crying in the crib. The overworked Polish farm woman often does not have time to 'straighten out the child' and certainly not to give it complete care. From now on it must depend partly on its older brothers and sisters, but mostly on itself.

THE CHILD GROWS UP

The Polish peasant child is a miniature adult. He does not live in a juvenile realm, with a child language and a childish freedom from care. He grows up in the world of his elders, sharing its reality and its responsibilities.

Only an infant is fondled, caressed, or called by a nickname. From the time he can toddle, the child is addressed by his full name and is seldom, if ever, kissed or petted. The period of babying seems to be prolonged in the case of the youngest child, but an older child who tries to demand the same kind of attention is ridiculed and told that *piesci c sie*, babying himself, is not dignified enough for his age.

The child in turn addresses his parents by the respectful 'you' rather than the intimate 'thou'. Any demonstration of feeling toward them is shown by kissing the hand or embracing the knees, rather than by flinging arms about them or kissing them on the face.

With this formality goes also a certain sense of dignity and a recognition that the child too is a person, with rights that must be respected. A Pole may speak more tenderly to his horse than to his son. But unlike many who lavish endearments on their children, he would never humiliate his son by beating or scolding him in the presence of an outsider. Nevertheless, Polish peasants on the whole remember their childhood, not as a halcyon playtime but as a time of hardship from which they were glad to emerge.

Status within the family is determined by age and sex. Even outside the family circle age must be respected always, regardless of social or economic status. Seniority among brothers and sisters is respected the more since children are made responsible for the ones next in line. Only babies are irresponsible and until 'baby comes into his mind' the older children are held to account for his behaviour, even though they themselves may be but four or five years old. They are as parents to their younger brothers and sisters, and these strong childhood ties often carry over into adult life. In folklore, the brother appears repeatedly as protector, guardian, and representative of his younger sister against a treacherous lover, a wicked stepmother, a cruel husband.

Females, except for the mother, have practically no voice in the management of the family or in family affairs. A girl is only a temporary member of the family, but the sons, depending on their ages, may express an opinion and even openly oppose the father, provided they show due respect. This is one condition that can never be violated without the condemnation of the whole community and a deep sense of guilt on the part of the children.

The child's sense of security is vested, not in the persons or the affections of the parents, but in the solidarity and stability of the family unit. He thinks in terms of the family as a whole and that is what he means when he says 'we'. The feeling of responsibility toward the family and the family property is engraved on children's consciousness very early in life, and it never leaves them.

While the general care of the children is in the hands of the mother, from the time they are about seven their discipline passes to the father, who applies it with a stern hand. The switch, the broom, and the belt are in common use. It is the duty of the parent to punish the children for their own good, for if the child lacks good disciplining during his formative years, he will have a hard life because he will grow to be a weakling. When an adult misbehaves he may be told, 'Your parents didn't beat you enough'.

The mother's hand is gentler than that of the father, whom most Polish children regard with distinct fear. The mother may serve as protectress, like the Virgin Mary with whom she often appears to be identified. Probably the warmest and strongest feeling is toward the mother in her protective role. The veneration for motherhood has been noted and it is believed that 'a hand lifted against one's mother will shrivel'. Yet she too is subject to the traditional ignominies and trials of old age, after the parents have retired.

During their formative years children often develop strong attachments to their godparents and grandparents, as well as to the older brothers and sisters who superintended their babyhood and who sometimes try to defend them from paternal discipline.

The Poles consider it good training as well as good management to assign definite tasks and duties even to the smallest children, making them responsible for the work and punishing them if anything goes wrong. Bringing up a child consists in a large measure of teaching him the various tasks that fall to his lot. Idleness is considered bad for him, as well as for the family that needs his services.

Each age has its characteristic occupation. Children of two or three can begin to help with those still younger, and this they will continue to do as other assignments are added. It often happens that a four-year-old boy rocks the cradle, feeds his little sister, and in fact does a large share of the household work while his parents are out in the fields.

By the time they are seven they are considered old enough to pasture the cattle. This is an important moment. So far the boy has gone about in a shirt held only with a belt, but now he gets trousers and perhaps a sheepskin coat. Girls also tend cattle, but from this time on they increasingly follow the routine of their mother, while the boys turn toward the father's work. For the first six years no differentiation is made between boys and girls, either in work or in play.

Cattle tending is a recognized stage in the child's development. To say to a girl, 'I knew you when you were still tending cattle' means 'I knew you before you were in your teens.' A child who is careless and lazy will be told, 'You are good for nothing, you will go on being a cattle-tender all your life,' and this is felt as scathing criticism. The progression of work through prescribed phases, and the role of the child in the domestic economy, are suggested by a popular lullaby:

Sleep, baby, sleep!
Or grow up
So that you may be useful to me
To guard the geese in the field, and then
To take care of the cattle
What's a little baby good for?

Tending cattle is a large order for a small child. They must go out early, sometimes at five o'clock, with little or no breakfast. Later someone may bring them food, since they cannot leave their charges. They are not free to move about or to play, for if the cow strays they will be punished for it. They live in fear of mistakes they cannot always avoid. Since instructions are given only in general terms, with no details, learning is done by trial and error. This helps to explain the feeling, so strong in Poland, that after a failure you can start all over again. The real defeat comes when one feels that he cannot try again.

Signs of intelligence and originality are highly approved. The child will be praised if he does a task in an unusual way, showing that he has been able to take command of the situation and to exercise his judgement.

At about nine or ten, a boy is considered capable of handling horses. The new dignity carries with it a rigorous ordeal, for in summer, when the horses work in the fields by day, they must be grazed by night. So precious a member of the family as a horse could not be permitted to wander alone at night, so the youth—who also works in the fields by day—is delegated to mount watch. Usually he spreads an old coat on the grass and sleeps uneasily with one eye on the horse who is tethered where the grass is lush. When the horse has eaten bare the plot that his long tether will allow him to reach, the boy moves him to a new spot and once again snatches some rest. Early in the morning the mosquitoes start to annoy the horses, and then they are taken home to supplement their all-night meal with fodder in the stable and perhaps to sleep.

If the return is early enough, the boy too may snatch an hour of sleep before going to the fields.

Sometimes a few boys get together, bake potatoes over a fire, and tell each other stories to while the time away. No food tastes better than potatoes roasted in the middle of the night, and the repertoire of song and story is limitless. Nevertheless, the occasional pleasures snatched during night grazing are negligible in comparison to its chronic pains, to judge by the reminiscences of peasants who tended the horses in their youth. They hated tending the horses, and the cattle too. They were separated from their age mates, unable to play or to move about freely.

While he is being schooled in his daily duties the child is also learning, through example and through precept, the personal credo by which he is expected to live. Key concepts in that credo are decorum, dignity and honour. These concepts overlap, and cover both morality and etiquette; in fact the two are felt as one, for the dictates of etiquette carry moral force and sanction.

Underlying decorum and dignity is the necessity for self-discipline. Much importance is attached to controlling mind and body, and to making the mind master of the body. Physiological and psychological demands are acknowledged only as they fit into the recognized scheme of custom and behaviour. No one can overstep these limits without being exposed to condemnation and ridicule. Body comfort, sexual desire, emotional needs must be repressed in favour of decorum. Eating and speaking, walking and even dying should be done with dignity.

The highest praise, especially for a man, is that he has strength of spirit, *hart ducha*. (In praising a woman one is more apt to say that she is a self-sacrificing wife or mother.) *Hart ducha* means a mastery of self that includes imperviousness to attacks on one's rights and independence. One does not flinch, one does not bend, one does not compromise, one does not fear, one does not surrender. 'Pawn yourself, but stand up', is a call to self-control and to courage.

Honour is the externalization, the visible proof, of all these virtues of *hart ducha*, the hard spirit. Accordingly it assumes tremendous importance and must be protected at all costs. It is involved not only in matters of life and death but in the details of daily living. When a person is humiliated or demeaned in the eyes of the world his honour suffers and he must defend it. For an individual to excel over his peers may also be felt as an affront to their honour. Honour is likewise linked with the rugged individualism that makes a *Voyt* ask politely for permission to enter a humble peasant's hut, and makes that peasant stand up for his rights against the *Voyt*, the *Starosta*, or the national administration.

Where honour and decorum are all-important, offence may be taken quickly and often. And where the restraints demanded and practised in every-day life are all-embracing and rigid, occasional relief is required. There are many socially sanctioned outbursts which provide the peasant with an occasional safety-valve. Holidays and family celebrations, Saturday dancing and parties, provide gay interludes. The peasant is thrifty and sober, yet a great deal of money and effort is spent on those occasions, with an elaborate and rich display of food. Very often that expenditure means starvation before the new harvest comes in, but it doesn't matter. A man has to feel like a king now and then, even if it is only for a day. There is singing and dancing late into the night, and of course brawls and drunkenness are a part of it. Fights are common if people from another village are present. The precipitating cause is usually that someone was insulted—a name was used improperly, a derisive song was sung, somebody implied something unpleasant. They exchange sharp words, gossip maliciously, fight and apologize. Then the air is cleared, everything should be forgotten and no further mention is made of the incident.

Shame—the corollary of honour and decorum—is a strong weapon in enforcing correct behaviour on children and also on adults. Babies are shamed if they are 'immodest', or offend the canons of good taste in defecation. Children are taught to be ashamed if any portion of the body is exposed, even to members of the family. Even to mention bodily needs and functions is disgusting. 'We Poles are ashamed of everything,' remarked one. An exception to the rule of physical modesty is that a mother does not hesitate to bare her breast and suckle her child before anyone, of either sex.

Parents consider shaming to be the most effective discipline of all, for major breaches. To be struck in sudden anger is punishment the child takes in its stride, little as he may relish it. More solemn and more agonizing for young people acutely sensitized to humiliation is the premeditated beating in the presence of the assembled family, especially if the offender is made to lie down on a bench and lower his trousers. It is the father who administers a premeditated whipping, and such discipline continues until the youth is full grown. These occasions, as intended, are long remembered. Undoubtedly—although this is not intended and perhaps not fully realized—such memories play their part in the grim drama that often marks the retirement of the parents after their sons have grown up.

Sexual decorum is a conspicuous part of the credo impressed on the child. Whatever verbal instruction he receives about the sex functions will not be from his parents, since the subject is taboo within the family circle. There is little danger of prolonged ignorance, of course, when the whole family sleeps in the same room; the stable and barnyard are free for observation, and the seasonal performances of stallion and bull are as well attended and as widely discussed as a small town circus. Moreover, outside the family sexual reference is uninhibited. Girls easily learn from their age mates what their mothers would never mention to them.

The great emphasis on feminine virginity before marriage has become somewhat formalized in recent years. A girl who has an illegitimate child is not necessarily doomed. Pressure will probably be brought to make the man marry her, perhaps even the *Voyt* will lend his influence. Failing marriage with the father, she has two possibilities. She may marry beneath her station, accepting a landless farmhand or artisan. In some communities all will be forgotten after a time. Elsewhere such a marriage might be considered worse than the moral stigma of illegitimacy, for the family if not for the girl herself. As an alternative to marrying 'beneath herself' a girl may go to work in the city, leaving the child behind and sending money home regularly 'for the bottle'. If she marries in the city her past may never be known and she may even never see the child again.

The penalty paid for illegitimacy by mother and by child varies sharply in different regions. In the lowlands the girl's parents will go to great lengths to conceal or adjust such a calamity. In the Podhale, where there is far less inhibition in all respects, such irregularities are taken more lightly.

The respect for property, deeply ingrained in the child from his earliest years, carries the force of moral obligation. His feeling for the farm is part of his feeling for the family. The father commands respect as an administrator of the farm, but he is only a temporary administrator. His authority will pass but the family property remains. To destroy property that represents much human labour—a beehive, or an orchard—is a worse crime than murder.

The lending of personal property is done with reluctance. It may bring bad luck and the lender must employ preventive measures. It is safe to lend to good people, friends and relatives, but dangerous to lend one's possessions to those who are bad, who are suspected of communicating with the devil, who have 'evil eyes' or 'unhappy hands'. It is also unlucky to lend on Monday or Friday, which are 'fatal days', or during bad hours.

When a housewife lends clothes, she gives them folded on the right side. They are returned folded on the wrong side. Kerchiefs worn on the head are not loaned because the lender would get a headache, and people prefer not to lend sharp instruments. Needles if lent are not taken back, because the needle is an unhappy object and when it returns it will break, or will prick one's finger.

The Polish peasant is probably the most polite and well mannered man in Europe. Children are drilled in good manners over and over from the time they are tiny, and are rebuked if they fall short of the standards of dignity. The word is used constantly in correcting their behaviour. Correct observance is far more strict in the country than in the city. In both, however, breach of etiquette is regarded as an insult, even between friends—that is, to be rude is to disregard the other person's honour.

Rural etiquette prescribes certain expressions and even certain dialogues for everyday life and it is not permissible to improvise substitutes. For instance, if a person passes people working in the field he should say, 'God help you'. When ploughing is being done, he asks 'Is it too wet?' When passing by shepherds it would be bad form merely to greet them with 'Praise the Lord.' One should ask, 'How does the shepherding go?' They usually answer, 'It is all right.' Another question may be added: 'Why don't you sing?' or 'Why don't you smoke?' No further conversation is necessary.

If a person comes upon a group of chatting neighbours, he should stop and show some interest in their talk. He may ask, 'What are you discussing?' Otherwise they would say,

'Look what an *honorowy!*' In this case, *honorowy*, or man of honour, is used as a sarcastic term.

When acquaintances meet, there must be a short dialogue after the customary greeting. For example: 'How is your health?' 'Thank God—and are you all right?' 'Thank God, little by little.' 'What news?' 'Nothing interesting, just old misery.' 'Better old than new.' The wealth of rhymed proverbs that besprinkle the peasant's speech figure largely in such conventionalized dialogue.

Even people who are very close to each other do not show heartiness in greeting or leaving each other. If they displayed the exuberant enthusiasm which is part of the conventional greeting in the United States, they would be regarded with suspicion.

In lengthy talks, as well as in brief exchanges, prescribed or stereotyped sayings are more frequent than free expression of one's feeling. Correct conversation is slow and guarded. The peasant is especially reluctant to open up before strangers. Personal questions are considered tactless and wasteful, and usually draw a stubborn silence. One keeps his feelings to himself, and away from the public gaze, although women are somewhat more free than men in their conversation.

Happy and cheerful people are assumed to be shallow and stupid, in fact gaiety and stupidity are often synonymous. 'He laughs like a dunce' is the common saying about a person who laughs a great deal without apparent cause, or 'he shows his teeth'. When people do not know what has made a person laugh they say, 'Who can guess what the idiot has on his mind?'

When children become too lively they are told, 'Who laughs too much cries later.' The general superstition is that 'singing on Friday morning will bring tears that night'. Excessive laughing and high spirits are reserved for great occasions. Otherwise people who are boisterous are accused of ignorance, or of not knowing how to suffer, or of having some secret source of happiness, probably evil.

People should not be too sad either. The best thing is to be mildly restrained, but sadness is tolerated more than unreasonable gaiety. When people meet they are more reluctant in telling of the happy events in their family than about the misfortunes. They are not expected to tell the whole truth in any case.

Children are taught restraint in all things. If they fail to curb their tongues or their tempers, they are punished with a severe beating. Complete physical relaxation is restricted to complete privacy. Good manners require that in company one should invariably be erect and poised, though not necessarily tense. Knees must never be far apart and seated women must keep them together. To yawn, stretch, scratch oneself, cross one's legs, is the mark of a boor. It is extremely ill-bred also to play with one's hair or comb it in public, or to show any consciousness of any part of the body.

A special point is made of restraint in eating. It is bad taste to show hunger or eagerness for food. No matter how famished, a person must eat slowly, occasionally putting down his spoon to show that he is master of his appetite.

Meals are eaten at a table only on festive occasions. Ordinarily a bench is pulled into the entry or outdoors, and the food is set on this, with knives and wooden spoons around the common bowl or bowls. Forks are little used—much of the food would require spoons in any case. Each person has his own spoon, which is rigidly reserved for his own use, and has its special place in a rack that hangs on the wall. There is some feeling that to use another person's spoon may bring pimples on the lips.

Children do not always sit at the table, but they may eat standing up except for holidays and special occasions. The grown-ups sit on the doorstep or on low stools near the bench, rest their right elbows on their knees, and reach into the common bowl. The head of the family makes a point of putting down his spoon from time to time to set a good example to the children. If a child misbehaves at a meal, he may be sent to eat in a corner, alone. He is never deprived of 'solid' food as a punishment, although he may lose a sweet if he is naughty.

Order of seniority is rigidly observed in eating. The head of the house dips his spoon into the bowl first, then the others in order of age. This is repeated in sedate rhythm, each dipping his spoon in turn with no unseemly haste or greed.

Food is neither forced on the children nor denied to them. When they have eaten their fill they put their spoons down on the bench and say: 'I've had enough'. A grown-up wipes his mouth with the back of his hand to show he has finished eating. Neither child nor adult would leave the meal without thanking the housewife for it.

Part of the eating etiquette taught the child has to do with guests. Guests at meals are rare, because most peasants have barely enough for themselves and even more because eating is an intimate affair, a biological function. One does not eat before strangers at all. If anyone comes in while people are eating, he gives the usual 'Praise God', and takes a seat at a distance from the table. If the host says, 'Come to us', and makes a place for him, the guest should not let himself be persuaded easily. He must hold out as long as possible and deny that he is hungry, even if he is starving. If finally he succumbs to wheedling, he must put his spoon into the bowl only occasionally, with the hostess constantly encouraging him. After the meal he must, of course, thank his hosts effusively.

In addition to encouraging her guest, the housewife would be expected to apologize for the poor food, while the guest keeps up a counter-barrage of praise. One must always apologize for one's home, one's food, one's possessions. If callers come, a woman will beg their indulgence because her house is not in order, and she will move about putting things into place—even if it has just been cleaned. While apologizing a person will, of course, set out the best he has, perhaps quoting the proverb, 'The house welcomes with what it has to offer.' Even a poor home will strain its resources to entertain a guest, both because etiquette demands such effort and for the sake of face. Rather than publicize his straits, a man would pinch and scrape to feed his hired help well, even though he himself might go hungry.

The great stress laid on etiquette by Poles makes them seem false to some outsiders. The Pole, however, feels that if he failed to observe etiquette he would be insulting you. To him such observance seems not insincerity but respect, and *he* is insulted if the forms are not observed toward him.

An example of response to breach of etiquette was seen when an ethnologist from the city went to study the village ways. The peasants received him hospitably and invited him to eat. The city guest required no urging but ate promptly and heartily, exclaiming at his hunger. The peasants were outraged at this lack of breeding. On the one hand, it marked the visitor as an uncouth boor, a social illiterate. On the other hand, it betrayed lack of respect toward his hosts, to treat them so unceremoniously. Accordingly the guest was cold-shouldered and his hoped-for sources of information 'dried up.'

The rural conception of etiquette is part of the larger conception that embraces the moral and the physical universe, making of them in fact a universe as compared to the multiverse in which the townsman moves. In learning the categorical imperatives of human behaviour, the child learns also to perceive himself as part of a stable, God-given order. This order applies to others as well as to himself—a saving

DANCING IN SILESIA

CORPUS CHRISTI PROCESSION IN LOWICZ

grace of the Polish peasant is his recognition that other people exist. He is fanatic in insisting on his own rights, but he also recognizes the rights of others, including his own children. He insists that others 'remember their place' but he does the same himself. He is feverish in taking offence at real or imagined slights to his honour, but he grants others the right to similar outbursts.

Whatever their actual source, all attributes of the peasant's universe are fitted into the teachings of the Church. Religion is learned as inevitably and as naturally as breathing. Prayers are taught to the children as soon as they begin to talk, but more of the religious education comes through imitation, observation, and participation than through deliberate instruction.

Children are taken to church regularly and a great point is made of attendance, not only for religious reasons. One obligation parents put into words is that they should take their children to church—and also to the fairs—'to see others and to be seen'. This is part of the process of proper social placement. The child has a right to social orientation; he and others must know his place and respect it. The Church is peculiarly fitted to impart social orientation, along with religious edification, for the order of seating at church provides a blueprint of the social structure of the village.

The teaching of religion was compulsory in all elementary and secondary schools until the second World War. Priests were state employees, paid by the national Treasury, and the Church was the biggest owner of land and buildings. It was supported by the government in every way, and its influence has permeated every phase of Polish peasant life.

Until recent years, formal education played a comparatively minor part in the life of the Polish peasant. Children went to school in a desultory way but illiteracy was exceedingly high in many regions, especially where the roads were

P

bad. There was not a school in each village, and in winter when they could be spared from the farm work, it was often too cold to go the long way to the nearest one—especially since many children had only inadequate clothing.

Even if they reached school, the teaching was far from competent. Rural school teachers were for the most part city people who had failed in other callings, so that incompetence and sadistic bitterness were almost taken for granted as part of the professional equipment.

If they did go to school the children had problems about doing their home work. At night the one small lamp was needed for household tasks—perhaps plucking fowl, or sewing. Then too, if the child took time off for school work, his lack of participation in home duties was resented. Consequently he would be beaten at school next day for not knowing his lessons. Nevertheless, school was welcomed as an escape from the greater rigours of home and a chance for social advancement.

Since 1918 there has been an increasing effort to educate the peasants, and illiteracy is less common among the young than among their elders. Moreover, corporal punishment is now forbidden in the schools. Nevertheless, real ease in reading and writing is rare, except among the few who have been singled out for special education. Even today many parents resent and mistrust the school influence, as weakening the authority of the home.

Those selected for special education are almost exclusively boys. Sometimes the older brother and sisters will pool their resources to educate a gifted boy for 'the easier life' meaning a white collar job in the city, possibly the career of civil servant. This means that he will go to the University. It also means that he will try to learn the speech of the city and to free his tongue from the quaint diction that differentiates the peasant from the city dweller, regardless of locality.

Most often the boy selected for special education becomes a priest. Every family longs to have one son enter the priesthood, for this is an infalliable means to bettering his status, and theirs. A priest is not necessarily beloved or personally respected. But his status, higher than that of a peasant although lower than the nobility, is impressive. He dines with the gentry. He is addressed as a gentleman, and his former associates treat him with deference. He leads the life of the privileged, free from physical toil and plied with gifts by his parishioners.

Some additional education is acquired by the boys who go into military service. Every boy is supposed to serve hi term, a necessity regretted equally by the boys themselves and by the family who needs their help at home. They dislike leaving home, dislike the city, and have little zeal for serving their country—to them the homeland means, not Poland in general, but the place where they grew up. Moreover, marriage must usually be postponed until after military service, and being away may interfere with plans for getting the largest possible share of the family farm.

The actual army experience may not be too unpleasant. Young men sometimes acquire new skills and new sophistication and come back feeling able and important. If they are thrown among city boys, however, they may be hazed unmercifully and teased about their uncouth ways and speech.

The average Polish child would find it hard to imagine a culture where play was considered the primary business of childhood. Nevertheless, Polish peasant children do have their moments of fun, especially during the earliest years. From then on, their pleasures, like those of the grown-ups, must be snatched between hours of work.

While the baby is still at the breast its mother sings it to sleep with numerous and delightful lullabies. When it grows a little older, she amuses it with verses, chanted while

swinging or tickling it, or counting its fingers and toes.
Stroking the child's hand, she recites:

> *Kitty, kitty*
> *Where have you been?*
> *In the pantry*
> *On the shelf, drinking milk—*
> *Scat, scat!* (*with a gesture as though chasing the*
>   *cat away*).

Or, stroking the palm and pulling the fingers, she varies
the following verse with imitations of different bird and
animal sounds:

> *Tiu, tiu, tiu*
> *The mother hen cooked some porridge*
> *She fed this one, she fed this one, she fed this one*
> *But she pulled this one's head off*
> *And fru, fru, flew away.*

Seated on someone's knee, the child is bounced to riding
songs:

> *The master comes riding*
> *The peasant behind him*
> *Hop, hop, on the horse*
> *Behind the peasant comes a Jew*
> *Ta-da-da, ta-da-da, ta-da-da* (*imitating hoofbeats*)
> *Here comes the master, the captain*
> *His servant behind him with breakfast*
> *Ta-da-da, ta-da-da, ta-da-da.*

Among the most popular games from the earliest years are
those imitating the activities of adults. A very small child will
lie on its back while someone lifts up its feet, holding them
together and swinging them from side to side imitating the
motion of chaff-cutting, with the words, '*Panu, panu, sobie,*
sobie—' 'for the master, for the master, for yourself, for yourself'.

When the children are old enough to play among themselves, imitations of adult work are still common. One game
shows the activities connected with raising and preparing
flax, to the accompaniment of a song:

Do you know how flax is sowed?
This is how flax is sowed?
Gathered, braked, etc., etc.

In addition to games centring around farm activities, chasing games and guessing games are popular, as with most children. In some the pursuer (fox, husband, or wife) prances outside the ring brandishing a cat o' nine tails, trying to break in and catch the pursued (chick, wife or husband). If he succeeds he is privileged to use the whip that he so often feels. A similar game, 'The Wolf and the Goslings' features a dialogue between the 'mother goose' and the 'goslings':

MOTHER: Go, goslings, go into the field.
GOSLINGS: We are afraid of the wolf.
MOTHER: Where is he?
GOSLINGS: Behind the fence.
MOTHER: What is he doing?
GOSLINGS: Raising a row. (Tearing cats).
MOTHER: What is he drinking?
GOSLINGS: Dishwater.

At the words 'catch the wolf!' all the 'goslings' rush out of the nest, and the 'wolf' seeks to catch as many as he can, carrying them off to his lair.

Until they are about six the boys and girls play together. After that, when they have begun working at different tasks, it is considered shameful for a boy to play with girls. Until they are about ten, they play in front of their homes, but then the boys take to the fields.

The boys have their special games, featuring warriors, kings, military camps and prisoners. Defeat may mean letting the winners beat the captured 'king' with their caps; or letting the 'king' beat the 'gypsy'. A girl's game, 'The Devil and the Angel', is a tug of war. If the angel wins there is kissing, dancing and general rejoicing. If the devil wins, all fight.

As the young people outgrow childish games, they find pleasure in social gatherings, and in the society of their contemporaries in their free evening hours, at church, at the fairs, and in the fields where they work and sing. The prohibition against mingling of the sexes lifts as they graduate into full adolescence. In the evenings they often cluster outside their homes for conversations punctuated by laughter and by the eating of sunflower seeds—their equivalent of chewing gum. Like the great American confection, the sunflower seeds relieve tension, give one something to do in empty moments, and offer opportunity to develop a formidable technique.

Young men and girls also meet and talk outside the church on Sunday, the girls demure in their best clothes, carrying a Bible and white kerchief, or perhaps a flower.

At the fairs, while enjoying each other's company, they receive informal education in buying and selling, a highly formalized procedure accompanied by handplay. The buyer puts his palm on the seller's right hand in a gesture called 'fasten down' and says, 'I'll give you this much', naming the sum. The other then performs the same gesture, putting his palm on the buyer's hand, and says, 'I want this much'. This may continue for an hour, each gradually approaching the other's price, and is an exercise enjoyed in itself by the principals and by their appreciative audience. 'Whether you buy or not', says the proverb, 'you can still bargain.'

If and when they finally agree on a price, they shake hands with a flourish, go to the tavern, and drink together the 'litkup' which makes their agreement as binding as a written contract. One never breaks such a contract, for this is the common law and even a man who might cheat a court ruling knows that it is inviolable. Even if he later finds something wrong with the cow he has purchased, he must hold to his bargain and make the best of it.

The young people learn also that in buying and selling the omens must be controlled. Some say that if milk is sold after sunset the cow will dry up. In Southern Poland a cow that is offered for sale is bound to her stake with certain plants which have the power to draw in the buyers. Even if the price is too high and bidding has already stopped, the plants might make the bidder change his mind and come back. It is well to deal with a lucky person in all transactions, and may be worth while even if one has to overpay.

They have already discovered at home that the animal to be sold should be taken out of the barn backwards, so that it will not be too homesick; and in the case of a young animal, so that the mother will not pine for it. Part of the animal— some hairs or, in the case of a chicken, a few feathers—must be left behind, for otherwise no more of its kind would be born on the farm.

The spinning or harvesting parties in autumn and winter offer further opportunity for social pleasure, and also provide much of the informal education in legend and lore. Story telling is an important feature of these gatherings. There is always some one outstanding for ability to tell tales of heroes, devils, saints and spirits—often an older person, perhaps a wandering beggar who has picked up wondrous facts and fancies on his travels. To delight or terrify an assembled company with songs and stories during winter nights is a recognized function of the beggars, and their repertoire of folklore and anecdote provides one of their claims to a place in the social sun. Younger people also add their share to the narratives, and sometimes they continue the entertainment all night, 'cursing the cock's crow that calls them to work in the morning'.

There are gatherings for dancing too, but of course, the social high spots are the big holidays and the preparation for them, and also the occasional weddings. A concentrated recital of social activities may be deceptive, however. The time between diversions is much longer than the time they occupy. They are occasional peaks in a level expanse of hard work and privation.

Declining Years

Among the apparent paradoxes of Polish peasant life is the contrast between the doctrine of devout respect for old age, and the ignominy with which old age is attended. Children of the most prosperous families are taught to show courtesy and deference to all old people, including beggars. Since so many old people are beggars, and so many beggars make holy pilgrimages, a sense of their sanctity often enhances the sense of respect for age.

Yet most old people among the peasants are stripped of all property and authority, in fact of any claim to respect except their age. *Dziad*, the word for beggar, is also the word for old man and for grandfather. The precise meaning it carries can be judged only by the context. This identification in itself suggests the significance of old age. To be old is to be dispossessed—landless in a society where land ownership is the foundation of status.

The retirement that reduces the farmer to a landless state is not a sudden act, but is forced on him gradually through the successive marriage settlements made for his children. When the last child is married he is left without land or home, unless he is one of the very rare exceptions either too prosperous or too independent to follow the accepted pattern. Now and then a man may delay the marriage of his children or may stand out against overwhelming pressure and keep a foothold for himself. Usually, however, the farm is too small and the man too human to permit such swimming against the tide of tradition and public opinion.

The strength of the compulsion can be understood only if one remembers that the family unit and the family property take precedence over any individual. The father is merely temporary custodian of the property and temporary head of the family. He will cling to his power as long as he dares, but he himself believes in the authority of the tradition and the public opinion that coerce him.

Moreover, it is a matter of personal pride as well as of family 'face' for him to marry off his children as promptly and as profitably as possible. This will be the measure of his success or failure.

The usual expectation is that the children receive equal or roughly equivalent shares, except that those who put in most work are felt to deserve most in return. Partly on this theory, the older brothers have a preference over the younger. If the farm is rather small, the older ones may try to buy off the youngest, or may pool their resources to get him a city education, with the hope that he will go into some other calling and set his share free.

There is no binding rule, however, that determines the share given to each child. Technically the father has absolute right to divide his possessions in any way he chooses. This paternal free will can be the source of uncertainty and also of tension among the sons. The system leaves room for conniving to win the father's good graces at the expense of a brother. How sure can a young man be that while he is away on military service, some advantage will not be taken of his absence to reduce his share of the patrimony?

Not only can the system result in hostility among brothers, but its influence on the father-son relationship is unfortunate. To the father his sons are instruments, however innocent, of his involuntary abdication. He will then be at their mercy. The Polish peasant is a proud man and the prospect is tragic —the more so since experience furnishes little ground for optimism about his prospects after retirement.

The sons, on the other hand, resent the father's power to

command their services until he is ready to give them their share, and to dole out as much or as little as he may choose. They too are Poles, with a flaming pride. They carry in addition resentment for years of harsh domination and of the unspared rod, according to the stern parental rule for bringing up children unspoiled.

It is small wonder that, once the tyrant is deposed, he evokes feelings more of vengence than of pity. Popular precept and the Bible say, Honour thy parents; so does the contract drawn up by the notary. But the spontaneous promptings of a rebellious heart counsel, now get back at him for all these wretched years!

A popular story seems to put the situation in a capsule:

There was a peasant who had an old father and a little son. One day this man's wife said to him, 'We must get rid of the old man, he is too old, he eats too much and does nothing, I don't want him around any more.'

So the man loaded his old father on to a wagon and carted him off to the woods to die. He took his little boy along to help. When they reached the woods they dumped the old man, wagon and all, on to a pile of leaves, and went back.

On the way home the little boy said to his father, 'Father why did you leave that wagon there? That is very wasteful! Some day I will need that wagon to carry you off to the woods.'

The father did not like this idea at all. So they returned to the woods and brought the old man back, and he stayed with them until he died.

When the parents have become pensioners on the charity of their children, the mother may fare better than the father. Her preferred position is not because she is better loved—although on the whole she is—but because she is more useful. A woman's skills tend to be better preserved than a man's. Even when her strength declines she can still help about the house and look after the children. Children are often closer to their grandparents than to their parents. Whispering together behind the stove they exchange confidences, and the children listen enchanted to long tales which only bore the older members of the family.

The contract stipulating what parents may expect from the children to whom they make over their property, is the proverbial scrap of paper in both senses: it is often ignored, and it often furnishes a cause for battle.

The Pole is notorious for frequent recourse to the courts, and it is significant that more lawsuits are waged within the family than against outsiders. Here again the element of paradox appears. Two relatives who are fighting each other in the courts will nevertheless band together against an outsider who attacks either one.

People go to court about their inheritance, about their honour, about cheating, about brawls. Often they go knowing they won't 'get anything out of it', just for the principle of the thing. Practical results may be achieved better by recourse to common law, court is a matter of the record. Peasants seldom bring suit, however, against a member of upper class—a *pan*—for they are convinced that this would be too unequal. The judge is also one of the master class, and 'a crow would not pick out another crow's eyes'. Therefore, they say, 'the law is for the *pan* and the jail is for the people'.

Because of their frequent recourse to the law, the public notary is an important figure for the peasants. They go to him to have a contract drawn up, to institute a lawsuit, or at times merely for advice. He is not a villager, but must be sought out in the town. They put on their best clothes for the expedition and treat him most respectfully, hesitating to sit in his presence because of respect for his knowledge.

They themselves acquire a good deal of familiarity with the law, and are sometimes able to give their lawyer shrewd tips. The peasants enjoy the whole legal procedure and like to speak out in court as well as to hear the lawyer speak for them.

The village invariably takes sides in any lawsuit and what the village decrees is far more vital than the court verdict. Honour or anger may be satisfied by the legal procedure, but court condemnation does not necessarily carry public opinion along with it. The court is made up of educated strangers, city people devoid of decency. What the village thinks is what matters.

A court decision in favour of parents protesting against breach of the retirement contract is not invariably observed. This the parents know when retirement is arranged, and it contributes to the bitterness of that hour when they step from power to helplessness.

It has been claimed that most of Poland's beggars in the past were parents who have retired. When a retired peasant does take to begging it is often to shame his children for ill treatment, but the revenge may become a boomerang. Neighbours and fellow villagers shake their heads, eyebrows are raised, but the storm of censure passes and the parents are out on the road.

The role of the beggar in Poland is, of course, infinitely superior to that of a beggar in the West, where the occupation is regarded as shameful and its practitioner is devoid of status. Actually, the word has a different connotation in Poland, but there seems no practical substitute. Until recently, Polish beggars were considered a functional part of the village population, although it was a floating part and changed constantly. Even today, when they are less numerous and less important, they retain certain recognized functions and some claim to human dignity.

One of their chief functions is to receive the generosity of householders, thus increasing their credit with heaven. It is holy at all times to give to the needy, and on certain holidays it is obligatory. Moreover, giving to beggars on certain occasions brings luck. On All Souls' Day, in former times, the beggars appeared in a group before the church to receive donations from the whole community. They lined up in two rows, and the women presented them with small loaves of bread. Prosperous peasants even today sometimes will specified sums of money to the beggars.

In return, the beggars pray for their benefactors and above all for the dead relatives of those who befriend them. Their prayers are the more effective since so many of them make pilgrimages to holy places. In addition, the beggars oblige with a multitude of songs and stories, chiefly about the lives of the saints. Before the days of easy communication they were greatly valued also as carriers of news and gossip, since they travel from village to village.

To be a Polish beggar does not necessarily mean that one is unwilling to work. On the contrary, some are only part-time beggars, and do odd jobs for pay, or work out in the fields during part of the time. There is also a custom which has become legal practice through long usage, known as *laskawizna,* or 'charity living'. This term is applied when a well-to-do peasant gives shelter to an old man or woman who is no longer able to do heavy work and has no family of his own to look after him. In return for this generosity the aged person does light tasks, such as sweeping out the cottage, rocking and playing with the small children and guarding the house in the owner's absence. Such benefactors are rare today, but formerly many prosperous peasants would give shelter to such an old man or old woman, known in the household as 'little grandfather' or 'little grandmother'.

Most beggars carry a staff and a bag in which they store donations. Naughty children are threatened with that bag— one of the first things a Polish child hears is that the *dziad* will get him if he doesn't behave, and will put him into the sack. It is popularly believed that the capacity of those bags has no limit, and a person who never tires of asking for things is called a 'beggar's bag'.

Sometimes the parent-turned-beggar will come home, bringing in the bag gifts for his children and grandchildren—food, or useful articles that have been donated, trinkets bought with the alms that were begged, holy images from the shrines to which pilgrimage has been made. Such visits, like the original adoption of the beggar's role, show a curious picture of boomerang revenge, as well as a pathetic clinging to the hearth and the family around which the peasant's world revolves.

DEATH AND BURIAL

The peasant is afraid of the dead, but death itself he views with resigned fatalism. A normal death in the fullness of years is part of the life cycle; it is so decreed. Moreover, his religion tells him that death is only the doorway to a better life. Old men and women calmly prepare for it, tell what should be done with their belongings and what clothes they should be buried in. Most old women make and cherish their own burial outfit, as fine as can be afforded.

Sudden, violent or untimely death, and long death agonies are a different matter. Unnatural death is deeply dreaded, for it is ascribed either to black magic or to divine retribution, and it gives no opportunity to make one's peace with God. The man who dies unshriven will 'fry forever in boiling oil', or suffer still more hideous torment at the hands of horned devils. One of the most dire imprecations is, 'May sudden death overtake you', and one of the most fervent prayers is for preservation from such a fate.

To die with dignity is extremely important—the manner of death matters even more than the funeral fanfare. The ideal is to die composedly in bed, with one's family gathered about and with the religious ceremonies administered fully and impressively. The funeral is nevertheless a matter of great moment. Contracts with tenant farmers, the landless *komorniki*, sometimes stipulate that if the tenant dies the landlord is obliged to give him an honourable funeral.

Many of the Polish peasant beliefs about death are common throughout Europe. The word is feminine in Polish, and death is most often thought of as a woman—usually tall, draped in white, and very thin if not actually a skeleton. She is not generally regarded as malevolent, but rather as a good-hearted spirit, obedient to the will of God—often against her own inclination—and capable of being begged off or outwitted. She may be directed to a victim by black magic, or be driven away. And there are many tales about imprisoning her so that nobody on earth could die. For example, once a man locked her up in his snuff-box for seven years. Nobody died and the earth began to complain that she could not carry so many people so God ordered the man to release death.

She warns of her approach by creaks or sounds about the house, but especially by the peculiar behaviour of animals. Dogs don't like her, and react to her presence or even her distant approach. Ravens and owls are regarded as messengers of death or misfortune, and a crowing hen is a sure sign of calamity.

Signs may also appear on the doomed victim—perhaps a 'bloom' or white spot on the nail of the little finger of the left hand; perhaps yellow blotches on the hands; or he may have certain dreams; or may fail to throw a shadow at the Christmas Eve feast. Such evidence is supplemented by the divinations practised on holidays and other important occasions. If a candle goes out during the wedding ceremony, either the bride or the groom will die; on Christmas Eve, New Year or Easter, if candle smoke trails when it should rise, death will strike.

When death finally comes, she knocks three times on the window, calls the person three times by name, and gives him the death blow, usually on the cheek. Or she may kill by simply standing next to him, though as long as she stands at his feet he cannot die. A story is told of a well-to-do peasant who had a bed made on wheels. When death approached, they turned the bed around and kept her at bay. One way to ease a hard death is to turn the bed so that the head is where the feet were.

Before the priest comes to administer final rites, the dying person is changed into fresh clothing, the bed is tidied and the room put in order. To ease his dying the candle blessed on Candlemas Day is put into his hand, and his rosary or prayer book if he wishes them. The family kneel in prayer, but if they weep it should be quietly, for a display of grief would make it harder for him to tear himself away from the world he knows.

Steps are often taken to help death along. Sometimes pillows and featherbed are removed so that the soul will not linger in them. Sometimes the dying person asks to be laid on straw on the ground, to avoid knots that might tie the soul to the body, and also perhaps to benefit by contact with 'the holy earth'. If an infant is dying hard, it is taken in its crib and placed with its head halfway out the door, to start it on its way.

At the moment of death, doors and windows are opened wide to permit, or rather to invite, the soul to leave. Some beliefs about the soul have been suggested in descriptions of the holidays, especially of All Souls and Christmas Eve. It is pictured as the breath or, in more condensed form, as a puff of fog; or it is imagined as a ghost or spirit. It is also identified with the shadow, and murderers who have no soul may be detected by their lack of a shadow. During life, the soul resides somewhere vaguely near the heart.

A CERAMIC STATUETTE OF ST. ANTHONY, KIELCE REGION

AN OLD PEASANT WOMAN FROM CENTRAL POLAND

Sometimes the soul is reluctant to leave the body, especially if it has been sold to the devil. Innumerable folk stories describe such sales and their outcome. Sometimes the devil is outwitted but more often he triumphs over anyone wicked enough to engage in such unholy barter. Knowing what lies ahead, the soul will not leave the body until the devil pulls it out with hooks and tongs. The souls of perjurers are torn through their throats with the devil's bare hands, amid the frightful cawing of ravens.

Even after it has left the body, the soul hovers near until the bell tolls for the funeral, or until the procession enters the cemetery, or until the priest intones 'Requiescat in pace'. The bearers will know the instant at which the soul finally departs, for suddenly the corpse becomes heavy.

Souls are seldom seen but often heard. They have their chosen haunts, indoors and out, and the living must be careful not to harm or offend them. If one hears a strange sound, he must exclaim, 'All spirits praise the Lord!' The soul will answer, 'I praise Him too.' One should then ask what it needs so that it may rest, and it will reply: a creditor must be paid, a wrong righted, an injury forgiven. One must always do what a soul asks and, if it makes no request, must at least say a prayer for its salvation.

Once death has occurred, weeping and wailing are almost a ritual requirement, and are taken as the measure of grief. The neighbours say approvingly, 'a sorrowing family'. Children who failed to mourn their parents with 'tender tears' would be regarded as unnatural. But parents are warned against grieving too deeply for their children. The legend is known in all Poland of the daughter who was condemned in the next world to carry her mother's tears about in buckets; and of the one who returned to beg her mother not to cry so much, for her grave was flooded with the tears.

Women and children are the loudest mourners. Men may

Q

weep and sob if grief is very deep, but without the uncontrolled screaming and wringing of the hands that is correct for the feminine and the young.

As soon as the soul, with the last breath, has torn itself from the body, one of the family folds the hands over the heart and closes the eyes so that the corpse will not cast a spell, weighting down the eyelids with coins. The mouth is closed so that the deceased may not tear his clothes with his teeth, thus becoming a vampire; or gnash his teeth and kill someone near him. Sometimes the jaw is tied to make sure that the mouth stays closed, for the sake of all concerned. Clocks in the house are stopped until after the funeral, mirrors are covered so that the dead may not see his reflection, and also so that the living may not see it, or behold the image of death.

Among the first to be notified of a householder's death are his cattle and his bees. The announcement is made by the new master, so that they will accept him and not follow their dead owner by dying themselves. Sometimes the orchard and farm buildings are also notified, so that they will accept the change in good part.

Word is sent at once to neighbours. The form of the notice varies, but it is usually carried by a messenger with a stick of some sort—a walking stick, a staff topped with a cross or death's head, a notched stick, a rod split at one end, or a branch braided into a circle at the end. People gather at once, partly out of curiousity, partly to pay one more visit to their neighbour before he sets out on his last journey. They will find the house marked, perhaps by a mourning flag at the gate, or by shavings from the coffin; or perhaps by a wagon overturned in front of the entrance.

The body is thought to retain sense and sensations as long as it remains in the house, and even for a time in the grave. Therefore in preparing the deceased for burial, he is treated as though he were still alive. No one may enter the room until he is fully clothed, 'lest he be ashamed'. He is addressed by name asked politely to give his hand or his arm, and 'this makes the stiffness yield.'

Reverence for the dead and desire to carry out his wishes are strongly seconded by desire to protect oneself and one's family against his ill will. Every effort is made to send him on his journey well content, so that he will not come back.

Everything connected with the last service to the dead should be done without stint or niggardly bargaining, as grandly as the means of the family will permit. The clothing must be in good condition and of good quality since it will be on display in the next world as well as in this. It must not have been worn by someone else, or the deceased will become a vampire and draw that person to his doom. Young people are decked out as for a wedding, and older ones are sometimes buried in their wedding outfits, saved for this occasion.

No knots are made in sewing for the dead, since they might 'hold his sins' and make penance difficult. Any clothing that rips easily is said to be sewed 'as if for the dead'.

Shoes receive contradictory treatment in different places. In western Poland they are put into the coffin if they will not go on the feet, to be used 'for the arduous journey'. Elsewhere only linen hose are put on, the explicit reason being that 'the Lord Jesus would not admit to the glory of heaven one proud in boots'. Perhaps another motive is to prevent the dead from walking around too easily, over rough ground or in cold weather. Contrary to the prohibition against knots, but in line with the effort to discourage wandering, the feet or merely the big toes or the thumbs are tied together.

The body is laid out on a bench, or on boards supported by chairs. Since the soul is believed to stay near the body during this period, provision is made for its comfort. Light, food and drink are set out. A chair is placed beside the body for the soul to sit on, a towel hung there or on the door for it to weep into; perhaps a white sheet draped in a corner and a holy picture hung on it so that the soul may have rest and cheer during its vigil.

The death watch, common to all European peoples, is known in Poland as the empty night, *pusta noc,* perhaps because much of the furniture is removed from the house but also because the night is spent in frivolity. Another name is the 'lamented night'. Like most ceremonies pertaining to the dead, the death-watch reveals the dual motive; to protect the deceased from powers that might harm him, and to keep him from harming the living.

The wake is kept by brothers, neighbours and friends, and by old men and women hired for the purpose. In addition to singing and praying by the body, these venerable mourners will add their prayers and tears to those of the family at the funeral. Their mortuary services are among the chief functions of the beggars, and are one reason why the calling is not wholly without honour in Poland.

The watch is kept from the moment of death until the funeral, but during the day the watchers are only a few old people. Singing is continuous from the time the body is laid out until it is carried beyond the boundary of the village, for it gives protection against evil spirits. In singing the psalms all must rise, for otherwise the corpse would rise. The old people's songs are about the soul—its fear on leaving the body, concern over its resting place, prayers for remission of sin, reproaches to the body that has led it into temptation and tried it sorely during life.

At night visitors and other watchers come, offer a prayer beside the body, then take some refreshments and help to pass the time with games and songs. The death watch may become very lively with no disrespect to the corpse.

Certain activities are forbidden while the body is in the house, or even for some time after it has been buried. Sewing and pounding would prick or harm the soul. In some places the cottage must not be caulked or whitewashed for nine days, for fear of sealing it up in some cranny.

Other prohibitions are to protect the living, since 'the dead person may be an evil spirit, stealing life and health, doing harm to people, animals, plants or even lifeless things'. In some places the house is practically emptied, in others only blessed objects are carried out, for in the presence of death they lose their holy power. Food is not left in the same room with the body and often not cooked in the same house, for the presence of death would make it spoil. Ploughing or fertilizing would not be successful while death is near. If a hen is sitting in the room—and in winter she might be—the eggs will not hatch.

The person who dressed the body must not set out trees, or they will never bear. Using the comb with which a dead person was combed will make one's hair fall out. In sewing a shroud one must not break the thread off with one's teeth, or they will ache. If shavings from the coffin were left about they could injure all who stepped on them, so they are burned or put into the coffin. If a mare in foal were harnessed to the hearse, the foal would either be born dead or die very soon. Oxen are sometimes used since they are sterile anyway. The driver of a hearse must not whip the horses, for that deadly contact with the fibre in the whip would blight the hemp and flax in the fields.

Scraps from the shroud, and the needle with which it was sewn are destroyed, to prevent their being used for black magic. Some say that if a pinch of dirt from an open grave is given to a person in a drink, he will sicken and die. Similar means may be used to induce drunkenness in an enemy, or to make one invisible.

Because of its great power, the deathly influence may also be used to advantage. Birds can be kept from eating newly sown seeds by burning a few shavings from the coffin over a field, or by sowing from the sheet on which the body was laid out, or by measuring the body with a stick and then putting the stick in the field. Vermin can be destroyed by pouring on the corners of the house the water in which the body was washed. Thieves may be detected and punished by putting into the coffin the duplicate, or a part, of what he stole. As the object rots the thief will dry up and when it is completely decomposed he will die. If the broom used to sweep out the death room is merely waved over the cabbage, the foxes will not eat it.

Dangerous as is the influence of the dead, various relics or even the touch of a dead or dying person may bring luck or wealth or knowledge. Most powerful of all, for good or for evil, are relics of those who met an unholy end, by sudden death, by hanging or by suicide. A piece of the rope, or better still a finger of a hanged man, will work wonders. Even a piece of his clothing rubbed on the watering trough will make cattle grow fat.

Many precautions centre about the coffin. No measurement must be made, but if it turns out too small the deceased will not find room in heaven and his family will wail, 'Oh the unfortunate! He suffered in life and now still must suffer after death!'

One must not haggle about the coffin, for the deceased would hear and his rest would be disturbed. It is wrong to order a coffin in advance except for oneself. The story is told of a man whose wife was mortally ill. Being more than normally thrifty, he decided to order the coffin in advance, fussed and bargained about it, and pestered the men who were making it. When the coffin was ready his wife recovered, but he himself died and was buried in it. He was guilty of three vices: unseemly haste in ordering the coffin, bargaining about its price, and fussing with the carpenters while they worked. The prohibition against niggardliness applies with equal force to all ceremonies and festivals. Disregard of it, as of any other custom, will be punished.

Relatives must not place the deceased in the coffin, since that would look as if they were eager to be rid of him, and also since the dead are especially dangerous to their own kin—he might 'attach himself' to them.

The custom of putting certain articles into the coffin is very common in rural Poland—provisions for the journey, objects cherished during life, articles that were borrowed or stolen and are apologetically returned. If the departed was fond of drink, an indulgent family will sometimes put a bottle of vodka into his coffin. In the Kracow region it is said he will return for his cap if that is not put in. The comb used on the body is put there, and the needle with which the shroud was sewn, sometimes broken 'so that it may not desire to sew another shroud'. Toys are put into the coffin of children, and perhaps gilded apples or flower wreaths, so that they may have something appropriate to play with in the meadow of paradise.

Money is included for several reasons: to use on the journey, for admission fee to heaven, to buy good fortune from the deceased, by way of restitution if one were in his debt, and by the heirs as legal payment for their inheritance. For one must not take anything from the dead under penalty of punishment. Failing proper payment, he may 'take his share' of the livestock by causing them to 'follow' him—that is, to die.

On the morning of the funeral, family, friends and neighbours gather to sing under the direction of an older farmer, and to bid a final farewell to the one who is dead. They take leave of him as if he were alive, members of the family kiss and embrace him, friends clasp his hand with words of good-bye. During all this there is loud weeping which intensifies as the lid of the coffin is nailed down.

The body is taken out feet first so that the deceased will not return, and the head of the coffin is touched on the doorstep. Or it may be put down three times on the doorstep and again three times on the outer step, each time with the prayer, 'Eternal rest give him, Oh Lord!'

When the coffin is on the wagon, all doors and windows of the house and outbuildings are flung open, and the lids of all chests, trunks, cupboard doors. Everything that closes is opened wide, to give the dead a last chance to view his home, and to make sure his soul is not shut in. In some regions the driver starts and stops the horses three times, so that the lingering and reluctant soul may break away and accompany the body.

As soon as the cortege is on its way, doors and windows are closed, and the chairs or bench on which the body was laid out are overturned, so that the soul will not come back. Another reason is 'so that the widow (or widower) may marry again'. The room is carefully swept at once, usually 'in the opposite direction'. The sweepings are thrown where no one walks, 'so that the soul won't be trampled into the ground', but also so that the living will not be contaminated. The house may be fumigated with juniper berries.

When the body is on the wagon, children and relatives embrace the coffin, weeping loudly, thanking the dead for all they have received, asking forgiveness for their faults and misdeeds. An older man then delivers the funeral speech, often known as the 'begging off', its theme being apology to the deceased.

The wagon carrying the body is usually the only vehicle, and the mourners go on foot. Priests and ministrants go first, followed by the wagon. Next comes the man who leads the singing, then the next of kin, followed by other relatives and friends, in order of their relationship.

At the first roadside shrine, the cortege usually stops for more praise and another farewell. In some regions near relatives accompany the body no further than this point, and only a few friends go on to the cemetery. The straw on which the body lay is usually thrown out here, or at a cross-road or a boundary line, to give the soul a place to rest in its wanderings.

The grave is generally dug after the body has reached the cemetery, by special diggers or by friends or distant relatives. If one wall gives way in the digging, it is a sign that the deceased was a miser; if water appears in the hole, he must have been a drunkard.

After the coffin has been lowered, with the head to the east, the priest three times sprinkles a little earth on it with the words: '*niech mu ziemia ziemia bedzie lekka*'—'may the earth bear lightly on him'. All follow suit, except in some places the closest relatives. Then all embrace the fresh grave and take final leave, saying 'Remain with God',—'*Zostancie z Bogiem.*'

No mourner must look back as he returns from the funeral, or there would be another funeral within a week. And they must move as quickly as possible, for evil spirits may be following.

On returning from the cemetery, all the participants are the guests of the family at the funeral feast, or *stypa*, usually in the house of the deceased. The *stypa* symbolizes both the economic status of the family and the degree of their grief, and the survivors strain their means to make it a rich one that will show due honour to the dead. A pig, a calf, or several geese may be killed and other luxuries offered, in addition to the foods traditional for funeral feasts. These traditional foods are also served at the Feast of All Souls: peas, *pecak*, and

noodles prepared with poppy seeds and honey, known as
lazanki.

As they eat, the mourners speak of the one who has died:
'A good man, may God give him rest'. One must never
speak evil of the dead. 'He shall be judged without our
judgement', they say.

Music, singing and even dancing are part of the *stypa.*
A slow *obertas* may be played during the feast, and in some
places a funeral dance known as *pogrzebowy* is performed. At
some point also, food will be given to the beggars—sug-
gesting, as does the whole series of funeral rites, the blending
of Christian and pre-Christian elements. In giving food to the
beggars, for example, the Christian virtue of charity and the
payment for prayers on behalf of the dead mingle with the
pagan practice of food offerings to the dead.

Settlement of the estate, if there is any, takes place on the
eighth day after the funeral. Despite the belief that the soul
of the deceased is present, seeing and hearing all, bitter and
prolonged disputes are apt to arise, often ending in the law
courts. The peasants' poverty is great, land is scarce and
precious, and close relatives wrangle bitterly over it.

Mourning usually lasts a year, after which a widow or
widower may marry with propriety. In practise, excuse is
made for a widower with small children if he marries before
the year has ended. During the period of mourning the
family refrains from dancing and amusements. The mourning
colour was formerly white, but black has become more common in recent years, and in some places both colours are
used. In any case, mourning clothes are not the rule among
the peasants.

Remembrance of the dead is long, however, the funeral
feast is often repeated at intervals, including the anniversary.
But aside from the *stypa,* the dead are remembered
frequently, often mentioned in conversation and in prayers,

special masses are said for them in church, candles are burned for them, their graves are carefully tended. On important holidays and at family events there is belief that they are present in the family circle. And always they are shown a deference blended of reverence and self-defence. Thus the peasant's belief in a life beyond this world insures a measure of immortality here on earth.

The history of Poland has been one of basic consistency and but superficial change. Throughout the centuries, her boundaries and her rulers have changed, but always the Polish people have felt an essential core has remained untouched. This has been true of all Poland and especially of the peasants who form so large a part of her population.

Whether, and to what extent, the life described in these pages will survive is unknown. But the strength of peasant convictions concerning human dignity and human rights may be expected to oppose even the most inexorable attempts to destroy them.

Also available from Hippocrene Books . .

POLISH CUSTOMS, TRADITIONS, AND FOLKLORE
Sophie Hodorowicz Knab
"This collection is a tremendous asset to understanding the ethnic behavior of a people. Highly recommended" —*Polish American Journal*
304 pages, 12 b/w photos & illustrations, 0-7818-0068-4, $19.95

POLISH HERBS, FLOWERS & FOLK MEDICINE
Sophie Hodorowicz Knab
A guided tour through monastery, castle, and cottage gardens, detailing over one hundred herbs and flowers and their role in folk medicine and traditions.
252 pages, illustrations, woodcuts, 0-7818-0319-5, $19.95

POLISH FOLK DANCES & SONGS: A Step-by-Step Guide
Ada Dziewanowska
The most comprehensive and definitive book on Polish dance in the English language, this work contains in-depth descriptions of over 80 of Poland's most characteristic and interesting dances, including such national dances as the Polonez and the Mazur, along with over 70 selected regional dances. All dances are accompanied by step-by-step instructions and illustrations, historical backdrops and musical scores.
800 pages, over 400 illustrations/figures, 0-7818-0420-5, $39.50

POLISH HERITAGE COOKERY
Robert and Maria Strybel
Julia Child selected *Polish Heritage Cookery* as one of the top fifteen cookbooks of the year on *Good Morning America*, also calling it "An encyclopedia of Polish Cookery and a wonderful thing to have!" —*Good Morning America*
895 pages, $35.00, 0-7818-0069-2

(All prices subject to change.)